Discovering God's presence in everyday life.

Andrew John Dumas

REKINDLING THE CHRISTIAN FLAME

Copyright 2025. Andrew Dumas

All rights reserved.

Requests for information should be addressed to:

Andrew Dumas

contact@andrewjohndumas.com

www.andrewjohndumas.com

New South Wales, Australia.

ISBN 978-1-7644158-3-5

No part of this book may be reproduced, stored in a retrieval system, or transmitted in any form or by any means, including electronic, mechanical, photocopying, recording, or otherwise, without prior written permission of the author, except for brief quotations used in reviews or scholarly works.

Cover design and Interior Design:

Jaime Hoare

www.creativefolkdesign.com.au

Thank you for opening this book.

The fact that you are here holding these pages, willing to pause, reflect, and wonder already speaks to a deeper longing within you. This book was written for moments just like this - times when we sense life is asking more of us, even if we cannot quite name it.

Whether you come with strong faith, a forgotten faith, or no faith at all, you're welcome here. There are no expectations other than being yourself. The invitation is to walk this path, to pause, to ponder, and to reflect on the deeper questions of your life.

This book provides an opportunity to explore the hidden and unknown aspects of life. Often, it's when we step back and take a moment that the spiritual flame is allowed to breathe through our lives.

I'm grateful that you've chosen to journey with me for a while.

Contents

1. Introduction — 5
2. Into the deep — 11
3. Calling — 31
4. Awaken — 43
5. Igniting justice — 57
6. Love in sacrifice — 75
7. The dark night — 91
8. Darkness cannot drive out darkness - Martin Luther Jr — 107
9. The road to authenticity — 119
10. Finding God — 141
11. Through community we ignite the Christian flame — 157
12. Discovering a life of simplicity — 175
13. Hope that brings a new beginning — 189
14. Conclusion — 203
15. Thank you — 207
16. Bibliography — 209

Acknowledgements

I am deeply grateful to my family, mentors, colleagues, and friends for their support throughout the writing of this book. Your encouragement, wisdom, and affirmation have sustained me. This work would not have been possible without your presence and willingness to go on the journey. Thank you.

Preface

The original motivation for writing this book was to reconnect Christians who might otherwise become disconnected from the church. In the last few decades, we have witnessed the falling away of many from the Christian faith in Western countries like the United States, Canada, the United Kingdom, and Australia. I believe that the Christian faith and Christian spirituality are a critical part of living a more whole and balanced life. As we journey through life, we can forget the important role that God plays in our lives.

This book is my attempt to reconnect us to our deeper selves, each other, and the mystery of the divine. This does not mean that I have all the answers, but rather that, through conversation, questioning, and prayer, we might discover something that was hidden. We have an opportunity to rediscover something deeper and sacred through the beauty and chaos of life.

About the author

Andrew Dumas is a husband, father, and teacher. He has taught in secondary Catholic schools for over 20 years. During that time, Andrew has served as a youth ministry coordinator, retreat leader, religious education coordinator, and adult formator. He believes that meeting people where they are at is a critical part of spiritual formation. Understanding a person's context and situation is essential to exploring their spiritual journey.

Andrew has also been deeply involved in Marist spirituality. The Marist spirit is Christian and seeks to follow Jesus in a down-to-earth, practical way, inspired by the example of Mary. Andrew has lived in several Marist communities and is an active member of Marist Way Australia, a committee of like-minded Marists, laypeople, religious sisters, religious priests, religious brothers, and missionary sisters committed to living out the Marist charism.

Beyond his professional and spiritual commitments, Andrew views being Christian as a call to live out the practical implications of what it means to be truly human. He believes it is in the present moment that we can attune more deeply to the fullness of life through the relationships we form. For Andrew, social justice is a vital pathway for encountering God in the ordinary rhythms of daily life. This book seeks to inspire others to rediscover God's presence in everyday life with a deeper meaning and purpose.

ANDREW JOHN DUMAS

If it feels helpful, consider praying this prayer slowly with me....

Dear God,
As we begin this journey to Rekindle the Christian flame,
we pray that You fill each one of us with Your presence.
Inspire us to look beyond what we see
to the deeper realities that often remain hidden throughout our lives.

May our experiences, especially the challenges and roadblocks,
become opportunities and doorways
into the tapestry of the divine woven through our lives.

Watch over us as we journey.
Guide us to walk slowly,
and lead us into a renewed journey with You.

Thank You for creating us.
Thank You for the invitation.
Jesus, our Brother, bless each one of us.
Amen

Chapter One

Introduction

When I was 14 years old, in the middle of winter, my parents allowed my friend and me to go camping. In Sydney, temperatures can drop to zero degrees Celsius, cold enough for things to start freezing. We didn't bring a tent, just our sleeping bags, some thick jackets, and his dog. We hiked from one side of the national park to the other. As evening approached, we set up camp on the edge of a cliff, not at a campsite. The top of the cliff overlooking the gully below would be a good, strategic spot. How wrong we were.

We didn't set up a campfire to keep warm. We didn't pitch a tent to protect us from the cold and the falling dew. All we had was each other. We lay on the rocks near the cliff's edge. As the night wore on, it got colder and colder. On a wintry Sydney night in mid-July, temperatures can drop below zero. The wind soon picked up , where we were near the edge of the cliff. We would have frozen, but for my friend's dog, who lay strategically between our bodies, keeping us warm.

We woke early the next morning to a thick layer of ice on our sleeping bags. Our bodies were shivering. We had learned the hard way. If only we had known to choose a better spot, to pitch a tent and build a campfire. But we had chosen the wrong location; a campfire on the cliff edge could have easily gotten out of hand. We didn't realise just how critical a fire might be.

When I was a child, my father used to build a fire in the backyard for a Sunday barbecue. He would send us kids out to collect small sticks and larger pieces of fallen wooden branches from the bush in our backyard, especially from the 200-year-old Australian gum tree that stood proudly near the back fence. Dad had a special technique for starting a fire. He prepared by crumpling sheets of newspaper into balls and layering them at the bottom of the fireplace. Then he might arrange the small sticks and twigs, angled upwards at the top.

He kindled the fire by lighting the paper underneath, leaving just enough space for air to flow through and help ignite the wood above. Sometimes the fire wouldn't catch, and we'd have to try again. But with Dad in charge, most of the time, a fire lit easily. Before long, we were cooking our barbecue, sizzling sausages and thinly sliced potato chips that Mum affectionately called "soddies." The fire gave the food a rich, smoky aroma. Occasionally, the smoke might blow into our eyes, making us tear up and want to avoid the sting. By the end, we all smelled like smoke. It felt as though Dad had initiated us into the ancient art of building a fire.

As the years passed, our local city council began to restrict the types of fires you could light in the Sydney metro area. At times, a complete fire ban was enforced, with gas barbecues being preferred over traditional wood fires. Slowly, my family began to lose the art of building a fire. The fading of that tradition is a paradigm of how my family started to lose touch with our Christian ways of doing things.

Other things took priority: watching movies on TV, chatting with teenage friends on the telephone. In the year 1992, we inherited a Commodore 128 computer (an advanced version of the 1980s Commodore 64 games machine). We had lost touch with simple, meaningful activities with Dad, like lighting a fire. When we entered our late teens, Mum and Dad started to struggle with getting us to go to church. It became just another obligation, something we had to do on Sundays. In a stern voice, Dad would say, "If you live in my house, you're going to church." However, we didn't understand the reasoning behind it. The deeper reasons behind going to church were never explained to make attendance relevant or meaningful.

Soon, there were more reasons to leave the church behind. By the 1990s and early 2000s, more cracks began to appear in the broader church. Scandals of abuse by some clergy and people with pastoral responsibility came to light across Western countries, along with the inadequate responses from certain bishops and other church leaders. Sometimes they preferred to move perpetrators on rather than hand the matter over to a civil court. The model of Church leadership had failed to prevent what could arguably be considered the worst crime against the most vulnerable.

As a result, in the decades that followed, the regular Australian national census showed many people were not identifying as Christians. There were voices that spoke up against these issues. Figures like Sydney auxiliary Bishop Geoffrey Robinson who advocated for the critical role of women in leadership to help prevent this, but these calls were largely ignored or silenced at that time.

The loss of trust and faith caused the Christian flame to dwindle, and the decline of Western countries like Australia and Europe led some to forget the meaning and purpose of God's beliefs and practices in their lives. Despite these and other problems that emerged within the church, God's invitation to be part of people's lives remains. However, Christian's own perceptions of the church and leadership, as reported in the media, did not seem to reflect a compassionate, listening ear; instead, they spoke of sternness and a rigid set of laws and rules. Many Christians began to equate the church with a harsh list of dos and don'ts, rather than a place of grace, dialogue, and welcome that accepted people where they were.

But the story of the Christian flame does not end there. This book invites you to rediscover something that may have grown faint, distant or quiet in your life. Sometimes guilt, shame or various obstacles can prevent us from recognising the Christian flame in our lives. Through the pages of this book, you are welcome to consider this journey woven through stories, reflections, poems, and gentle prompts, each one designed to help you pause, look deeper, and recognise the sacred presence already at work within and around you. This space helps you notice that in ordinary moments, God never stopped working.

Your commissioning...

This book is structured with a series of questions at the end of each chapter, inviting the reader to pause and take time before moving on. You are encouraged to write and journal, using a pen and an exercise book for journaling, as a spiritual tool to reflect on your own lived experience. I believe that God is hidden in the fabric of your life, so this process seeks to help you notice and name those sacred threads. Set aside a time, whether in the morning, evening, or during the day, to be fully present, to ponder, and write about your life. Please be open to this process. By reading, journaling, sharing, and through prayer, you are invited to respond and become part of that conversation. Give yourself a day, or even a week, before beginning the next chapter. This is a journey of formation, one that, if entered with intention, provides opportunities to live life more fully attuned to that sacred presence.

At the end of each chapter, and after your journal entry, take time to pray.

Slowly... ever so slowly, pray the prayer intention.

God never forces God's way into a person's heart.

Through reading, reflecting, in stillness and with conversation, the reader may rekindle the Christian flame.

This process is not about finding the correct answers. Instead, it is about having the grace to stop, to take the time, be yourself, and allow God to speak to you in ways you do not expect.

Finally, Jesus sent his disciples out in twos (Mark 6:7). Never alone. I encourage you to read this book with at least one or two other people. Read together. Reflect and journal together. Discuss and ponder together. Pray together. Choose others to accompany you on this spiritual journey to Rekindle the Christian Flame. Pause and pray together. Jesus said, *"Where two or three are gathered, there I am"* (Matthew 18:20).

Chapter Two

Into the deep

Reflection - into the Deep

"*I brought my son to the ocean's edge,*
 When he was one,
Thinking that this would be fun.
With the waves,
With water,
With sounds,
With the sand.

I took my son to the water's edge,

His feet to paddle and play in the sun.
But gloomy clouds soon arose,
And fear became my son's drum.

Tears turned day into night,
Waves,
Twisting and turning,
Crashing and booming,
Both inside and out.
My son,
No longer wanting to go to the water's edge,
Wished to stay far from the ocean,
For fear-waves had now entered his heart.

The waves,
Of twisting and turning,
Were no longer fun." (The author)

We are "water people". We are deeply connected to water. Without water, humanity would not survive. Water makes up most of the human body. We are drawn to it, drawn to the ocean. The ocean reflects who we are. Whether we live by the ocean or visit it, it can stir wonder within us. There is a deep beauty in watching something so powerful, so alive, constantly moving and stirring. That same movement exists within each of us, a stirring of great beauty, but also of great terror. The emotional ups and downs, or the encounters of conflict or bliss between those we love, can reflect the waves of the ocean in our own lives.

Our lives are like journeys across vast oceans. Sometimes, the oceans are peaceful and still, reflecting the sun's awesome radiance. The sky turns shades of blue and emerald green. We often struggle to find words to capture the elegance and exquisiteness of the ocean. Though we feel its beauty deeply in our hearts, we often struggle to convey its brilliance when we return home.

On the other hand, rain clouds gather. Great storms can arrive, blocking out the sun. The mood and the power of the ocean shift. It turns dark, threatening to destroy everything in its path. Waves rise as powerful instruments of nature. Boats struggle to survive as the waves tower, sometimes many metres tall above them.

The spiritual boats we travel on in life can reflect many different kinds of storms and terrors. For some, leaving the boat, jumping overboard, or getting off at the next port may be a way to get through the storm. Recent public inquiries and scandals involving clerical sexual abuse have been the catalyst for many people losing faith and leaving the Church. Many disillusioned Christians have lost faith and trust in the very people they once looked to as spiritual guides, the ones who told us from the pulpit to put out into the deep and let down our nets. For many, the way forward, and perhaps for us too, may seem to lie in a safer passage without the Church.

God does not stand off in the distance, hoping that we will work everything out on our own. Christians believe that God entered into the messiness of our human condition. God did not just want to know us; God wanted to participate in the movement that we call our lives. Not only in our joys and happiness, but also in our pain and sorrow. But where is God in the suffering we often face? If God is so powerful, why didn't God stop the sexual abuse of children? Elie Wiesel, a Holocaust survivor who wrestled deeply with the silence of God during the Holocaust, recounts witnessing the hanging of a child. In that moment, someone cried out, *"Where is God now?"* (Wiesel, p. 65, 2006). Viktor Frankl, also a Holocaust survivor, responded to this kind of anguish by suggesting that "Where is God?" may not be the right question. Instead, he asks, "Where is man when we face great suffering?" (Frankl, p. 66-70, 2006). Did God really choose this suffering? Or did human beings play a significant part through their own free will? These questions can lead us to wrestle with the existence of God, and to wonder whether the Church is truly divinely inspired.

What role does free will play when we are confronted with suffering? Viktor Frankl argues that each person is free to choose their response to any situation, no matter how painful or unjust it may be. When we think of God, we might imagine a powerful figure like Zeus, the Greek god, hurling lightning bolts from the sky, full of control and might. But in the Christian story, this is the exact opposite of what we perceive as the truth. God comes to us not in dominance, but in vulnerability, in the form of a fragile baby. God enters our lives through our powerlessness, the opposite of what many expected. God is the one who hangs on a tree, dying on the Cross. In the Christian story, God speaks more fully through human weakness than through displays of power and control. And this challenges us to see suffering not as a sign of God's absence, but as a place where God may be present and maybe revealed.

The apostle Paul writes:
"Though he was in the form of God,
He did not regard himself as equal to God.
as something to be grasped,
but emptied himself,
taking the form of a servant,
being born in human likeness.
And being found in human form,
He humbled himself

and became obedient to the point of death,
even death on a cross."
(Philippians 2:6–8, NRSV)

How can God allow so much human suffering to occur?

The Holocaust is one of the most tragic and horrifying examples of the misuse of human freedom. How can we ever justify the killing and abuse of innocent people, especially children? We cannot. And yet, amidst this darkness, there are stories of courage and compassion, people who risked their lives to save others.

One such person was Angelo Roncalli, who later became Pope John XXIII. While stationed in Istanbul, Turkey, during Nazi occupation, he risked his life to save over 600 Jewish children by issuing false baptismal certificates. He then arranged transit visas to help them escape to Palestine. Saving a life in the face of great evil or suffering is something deeply Christian.

At the beginning of Jesus' public ministry, He stood in a Jewish synagogue and read:

"The Spirit of the Lord is on me,
because he has anointed me
to proclaim good news to the poor.
He has sent me to proclaim freedom for the prisoners.
and recovery of sight for the blind,
to set the oppressed free,
to proclaim the year of the Lord's favour."
(Luke 4:18–19, NRSV)

Wherever there is injustice, our human relationships become even more important: we cannot stand idly by and allow evil and suffering to continue. When there is an injustice, we all suffer in different ways and struggle with many challenges, such as mental health, poverty, homelessness, environmental destruction, refugees fleeing war, or even domestic violence close to home. Each of us has our own demons or dark storms to face at some point in life. Human suffering reminds us about our shared humanity and the deep connection we have to one another. God does not avoid human pain; God enters into it. Jesus is scourged, crucified, and executed. There is something deep within us that pleads for such injustice not to be true. Surely, this cannot be God's design. The Prophet Isaiah stated the servant of God's role is: "to proclaim freedom for the prisoners and set the oppressed free." In times of great suffering, God calls us to act, to bring light into the darkness and hope into despair. We cannot stand alone, and neither does God.

How do we sense God?

Are we willing to step into deeper water? In the Christian baptismal rite, that is exactly what Christ invites us to do: to step into the water and be baptised. But this is not, in fact, a one-time event that may have happened to us as a baby or a child. God continually invites us to enter more fully into our lives, to step into what seems unknown and dark. Like an ocean. By stepping more fully into the waters of our own lives, we open ourselves to experiencing God more deeply.

God wants us to encounter a richer reality through our senses, what we taste, hear, see, and touch. Yet, as the anonymous author of The Cloud of Unknowing reminds us, *"God is ultimately beyond human comprehension and sensory perception"* (The author of the Cloud of Unknowing, p34-37, 2005). While our senses help us experience God's creation, they cannot truly grasp God's essence. How do we come to terms with the mystery that God became human? In truth, we cannot fully comprehend it. There is always an element of uncertainty and mystery that envelops our faith. The Incarnation, God becoming human in a particular time and place, offers us a glimpse of the divine, a glimpse of who God is.

A glimpse of who God is. If you had been alive in Palestine between 4 BCE and 30 CE, you could have encountered God through Jesus as a baby, a teacher, or a man who suffered and died. And yet, many people did not recognize Him. Much of that time, they could not recognise God in human form. So, what makes us think we would recognize God today, when so many failed to recognize Him in human form? The modern theologian James Finley speaks of fleeting experiences or small insights of God's presence (Rohr, Finley, & Bourgeault, 2010). On our spiritual journey, we may be blessed with sudden illuminations of God, like lightning flashes: brief, brilliant moments of grace that appear and disappear in an instant, like lightning that flashes across the ocean. These experiences cannot be forced or controlled. All we can do is open ourselves to the sacredness of the present moment, to step into the deep, and trust that God is already there, waiting.

Martin Luther introduced the concept of Deus absconditus, or *"the hidden God,"* suggesting that God's hiddenness can lead believers to seek Him more earnestly (Luther, p139-142, 2005). Later, imprisoned in a Nazi concentration camp, Dietrich Bonhoeffer reflected on the hiddenness of God in times of suffering, proposing that such experiences can lead to a more authentic and mature faith (Bonhoeffer, pp. 360-370, 1997). Suffering can cause us to question, "Is there a God?" Conversely, it might lead us to reach out and cry, "God, help me." Is this sensing God, or is it desperation, wanting God to be there?

In the modern Gospel interpretation of the television series The Chosen, spanning Seasons 1-4, we witness the development of a loving relationship between Thomas the Apostle and a young Jewish woman named

Ramah. Ramah decides to follow Jesus after witnessing His miracle at the Wedding of Cana. As their relationship grows, Thomas and Ramah eventually ask Jesus for permission to marry. Shortly after, Ramah is tragically killed. In his grief, Thomas begins to doubt Jesus and asks, "Why did You allow Ramah to die?" There is no easy answer. Yet the loss of Ramah reveals a deeper truth: our reasoning and our senses alone cannot understand what is happening. The prophet Isaiah writes, *"For my thoughts are not your thoughts, neither are your ways my ways,"* declares the Lord. *"As the heavens are higher than the earth, so are my ways higher than your ways and my thoughts than your thoughts"* (55:8-9). It is hard to come to terms with things that seem challenging, difficult, and even disastrous. We think these things should not happen.

After the resurrection, Thomas the Apostle hears that Jesus is alive, and he says, *"Unless I place my fingers in His side, I will not believe"* (John 20:25; NRSV). Later, Thomas physically places his finger into Jesus' side. This is not an illusion; Thomas, who doubts, changes his mind because of a tangible, physical encounter. Jesus responds, *"Because you have seen me, you believe; blessed are those who have not seen and yet believe"* (John 20:29; NRSV). We can come to know God through our senses alone. The absence of God often points us toward something more than who we are. Beyond our taste, touch, sight, sound, smell, emotions, and intellect. God is both within the human experience and beyond it. As the Nicene Creed says, God is "visible and invisible."

We must be careful not to place our faith solely on our own expectations or miracles to prove God's power. God's presence is often disguised in the ordinary, in the simple things of our life, present not with spectacle and glamour but in earthiness as an infant child. The Incarnation, where God became a person, teaches us that the world is sacred, and so is our own life. The ordinary is more important than we often realise. It can teach us how to be more fully alive. When we learn to see the extraordinary within the ordinary, we begin to discover God hidden in the everyday, not as a magician who waves a wand to solve all problems, but as a quiet presence calling us to participate in the divine image. In the ordinariness of our lives, we are invited to play a role.

Consider three stories:

At 14, John felt as if he were constantly drowning in a sea of expectations. School was overwhelming, his thoughts raced with anxiety he couldn't control, and the teasing from classmates about how he looked, and his faith made him feel ashamed. He had prayed with his dad for strength, for something to change, but all he seemed to receive was silence. Slowly, he stopped believing, skipped the beach family trips and picnics he used to love, and retreated into the world of computer gaming, where no one judged him, and he could be anyone he wanted to be. It felt easier to hide behind a screen than face a world of judgment.

Consider Craig's story:

Craig stared at his reflection in the cracked mirror, eyes hollow and rimmed with the weight of too many nights lost in the battle within. Addiction had subtly crept into his life quietly, disguised as relief, then comfort, then necessity, until it stole his ambition and motivation, fractured his relationships, and left him clinging to the ruins of who he thought he was. Each morning came with promises to stop, but the ache inside him always seemed louder than his resolve. He wasn't proud of the pretending, the regrets, or the shame in his own eyes.

And finally, Helen's Story:

At 80, Helen moved quietly through her days, the rooms of her family home echoing with silence and memories that no longer kept her warm. Since her husband passed and her children grew distant in their own busy lives, loneliness had settled in like a familiar shadow, and depression pressed against her spirit with each sunrise. She often stared out the window at the community garden across the street, watching the laughter of others, wondering if it was too late to join in, too foolish to begin again. Voices whispered that she didn't belong anymore, that new beginnings were for younger people.

Each of these stories paints a very different picture at different points in our lives. They show how we can become separated from life and the opportunity to step more fully alive into each moment, more fully alive. The culture of individualism paints a picture of us needing to fix the problems we face ourselves. Leading us to ask questions such as, can we free ourselves from the pains and struggles we face? Alternatively, is that the right perspective and way of seeing things? Is there a way we have not yet considered?

Are we called to take a leap of faith?

In the Gospel of Luke (5:1-11), before Jesus calls Peter, Jesus asks his small fishing boat to be put out into deep water and let down his nets to catch fish. Peter, an expert fisherman, has been fishing all night without success, yet now Jesus the carpenter, turned rabbi, is instructing the fisherman. The request is unusual and unexpected. There is a sense of confusion and disorientation, as if the seasoned professional is being taught by someone who clearly is no expert in fishing, or so it seems. The surprising outcome of the miraculous catch of fish was a turning point for Peter, But this story is not just about catching fish: it's about how we approach things that are beyond our control. Do we trust? Are we accepting? Are we open?

In her book Daring Greatly, the social researcher Brené Brown (2012) encourages us to lean into vulnerability, to lean into the things when we cannot control, to trust when we cannot see a way through, to face the parts of our lives that frighten us the most. This means shifting from controlling the steering wheel of our lives, which could be termed as a closed mindset, to allowing someone else to take the wheel. This seems to be a more open-minded set.

We need to step outside the stories we keep telling ourselves. Stories like, "I won't succeed if I try something new" or "I know best". Changing the internal narrative can change how we approach life. Our peers, who often face similar struggles, can only guide us so far. And while our parents may be well-intentioned, they, too, can only take us so far, because true spiritual growth often requires moving beyond the safety of our homes and what we know. Life is full of narratives, stories we tell ourselves. Some that serve us, and some that hold us back. Sometimes it takes a major life event like a classmate's death or suicide, a cancer diagnosis, or the loss of a job to shake us out of how we think and approach life. But what is needed in those moments is more than just a change in values or viewpoint.

A new way of being

We can be overwhelmed by the amount of information we receive each day. Our culture encourages us to be captivated by entertainment, pleasure, and whatever feels good in the moment. Surrounded by noise and stimulation, we begin to lose a sense of what is meaningful from what is merely desirable. Our culture trains us to seek the superficial, and we are entranced by what our desires want. We constantly scroll on our phones, play the next computer game, or check our social media updates for the twelfth time today. In this confusion, we lose a sense of what wisdom truly is, as we are not accustomed to the language of seeking deeper meaning. We remained trapped. Rarely pausing to look over our shoulders to consider what we are missing.

Do we need to learn to listen in new ways? Listening is like a tuning fork brought near another tuned to the same pitch; they begin to resonate and sound in harmony. Do we need to resonate with a different or new pitch? Do we acknowledge that we are out of tune with the pitch that is being played? If we acknowledge our inability to hear spiritual truths and wise words, we begin to tune into how to listen more actively and attentively.

Goodness, at first glance, is not always entirely good, because our perception of goodness can limit our growth. Our successes, or the thinking that we know best, can have a way of shutting the door to new beginnings. We might experience pleasure, money, riches, an "A" on an exam, power, a big prize in winning a large sum of money at a lottery, or feed our addictions with what feels good, but this is like a circle spinning on an old vinyl record, stuck with a scratch right through the middle that we choose to ignore. The needle gets caught, repeating the same part of the track. We long to take the record off, but we choose not to because it is good.

Conversely, in difficult times, when life seems to fall apart, such as after a heated argument with a loved one or a colleague, or maybe when things do not go our way, we can be overwhelmed by emotion, which prevents us from trying something new or tuning in. Like a toddler whose toy has been taken away, our world can crash down. Our emotional landscape floods, colouring the entire story of who we think we are. Just as good times can dull our spiritual awareness, bad times can also shut us off because we simply don't understand them or know why.

Given these circumstances, we may need a new way forward, because our old ways no longer seem to work. When the angel appeared to Mary in the Gospel of Luke, *"Mary is deeply troubled and confused. Mary did not know fully what was then in her life"* (1:29). *"But Mary kept all these things, pondering them in her heart"* (2:19).

Often, in our own lives, we feel confused and uncertain when presented with a new way of seeing things. In these moments, our instinct might be to run away, just like Joseph, Mary's engaged husband, because after hearing that Mary was pregnant, he thought of divorce. Perhaps Joseph thought, "She must be carrying another man's child?" But something deeper interrupted his plan. A dream from an angel telling him what had happened. This dream radically changed the direction of how he understood things and his decision, leading him to do the complete opposite of what he was thinking and feeling. He chose to stay. He chose to marry Mary. He chose to listen with an open heart.

Similarly, Joseph steps into the very situation that he fears. Marrying a woman already pregnant in first-century Jewish culture would have been a great scandal. Joseph acts despite a great scandal and doubt. The words *"do not be afraid"* occur more than 300 times in the Bible. Joseph's dream was not just a once-off event. In Matthew's Gospel, Joseph is depicted as having several dreams. Each dream asks Joseph to move away from what is familiar:

"Now after they had left, an angel of the Lord appeared to Joseph in a dream and said, 'Get up, take the child and his mother, and flee to Egypt, and remain there until I tell you; for Herod is about to search for the child, to destroy him" (Matthew, 2:13, NRSV).

Later, the angel invites Joseph to return:

"When Herod died, an angel of the Lord suddenly appeared in a dream to Joseph in Egypt and said, 'Get up, take the child and his mother, and go

to the land of Israel, for those who were seeking the child's life are dead.'" (Matthew 2:19-20, NRSV).

And finally, to settle in Galilee:

"But when he heard that Archelaus was ruling over Judea in place of his father Herod, he was afraid to go there. And after being warned in a dream, he went away to the district of Galilee" (Matthew 2:22).

In the modern context, dreams are often seen as psychological manifestations of what is happening in our lives. We can dream in symbols that reflect deeper aspects of our lives. But Joseph's dreams are presented as signs. God is communicating something through a message. However, maybe there is a symbol in these dreams also? Each dream demonstrates Joseph trusting the angel. Trust requires a person to let go of our control or way of seeing things and recognise something greater than the self or way of seeing things. Joseph's ability to listen brought about new choices and a new life for Mary and Jesus.

Similarly, to Joseph, are we today willing to trust and listen beyond what we expect? This seems rather scary. But this is precisely where Mark's Gospel begins:

"Now after John was arrested, Jesus came to Galilee, proclaiming the good news of God, and saying, 'The time is fulfilled, and the kingdom of God has come near; repent, and believe in the good news.' (Mark 1:14-15)

In English, we have translated *"repent"* as a religious word. But in the original Greek, when this Gospel was written, it meant so much more. The Greek word "μετάνοια" (metanoia) literally means *"a change of mind"*. But not just our mind, but our heart and our whole body. Furthermore, the word *"believe"* is often paired in the Gospels. The Greek word for believe "πιστεύω" (pisteuō), means to trust.

Later, trust plays an important part when Jesus calls out to Peter in a storm:

Peter answered him, "Lord, if it is you, command me to come to you on the water."
He said, "Come."
So, Peter got out of the boat, started walking on the water, and came toward Jesus.
But when he noticed the strong wind, he became frightened and, beginning to sink, cried out, "Lord, save me!"
Jesus immediately reached out his hand and caught him, saying to him, "You of little faith, why did you doubt?" (Matthew 14:28-31)

Are we called to go into the deep like Peter? When Peter began to sink, Jesus reached out and took his hand. Do we take Christ's hand when we sink? Do we seek the signs that help us to tune into the deeper rhythms of our own lives?

We are navigators of our own stories, but God invites us to move beyond the small fishponds of our backyards and embrace the vast ocean that shapes the whole world. We may be afraid of stepping into the ocean. It may seem dark, powerful, and beyond our control. Yet in 1492, if Christopher Columbus had not ventured into the unknown, sailing his boat off the edge of the ocean and beyond the horizon from Europe, he might never have discovered that the world is not flat, but round.

We are invited to go into the deep and resist staying in the shallowness of the noise or what might distract us. This takes a conscious effort to tactically step into moments that build meaning in our lives. The calming seas or the violent storms might be places where God is revealing a deeper meaning to us. True discernment might come through striking moments like powerful dreams or sudden insights, but it often grows through the ordinary experiences of our journey. We can attune to these moments by stopping and taking the time to ponder and consider each moment. Journaling can help create a routine that causes us to ponder more deeply. We need to ask: where is God hiding, and what can these ordinary moments teach us? In our world of constant distractions, this path of depth requires us to deepen our faith. That beneath the waves of confusion in our daily living, there is a presence already within us and around us; we need only step into the deep and attune to the mystery of our lives as it unfolds.

Journal

Spend 20 minutes journaling about the following.

Choose ONE of the following questions to journal about

1. God often speaks through silence, ordinariness, or even pain. When have you experienced God's presence in subtle or unexpected ways?

2. The quote, "Where is man when we face great suffering?" shifts the focus from God to human responsibility. What is one injustice in the world that calls you to action rather than to silence?

3. "We need a new way of being." What old habits, beliefs, or mindsets might you need to let go of to become more open to the movement of God in your life?

Journalling

Journalling

Journalling

Journalling

Prayer

Take a moment to pause.
   Close your eyes for two to three minutes.
   Become aware of your breathing.
   Breathe slowly.
   As you breathe in and as you breathe out.
   Afterwards, if it feels helpful, consider praying slowly this prayer in the days leading up to the next chapter.

Loving God,

Thank you for being with us, especially when life feels confusing or scary. Help us to listen with our hearts, not just our ears, so we can hear You in the quiet, in the silence, and in the ordinary moments of our day. Give us the wisdom to reflect and ponder like Mary and the courage to try new things like Peter, to care for others like Joseph, and to trust You even when we don't understand everything. When life feels shallow or distracted, lead us to go deeper, to discover Your presence in the stillness, in our struggles, and in our love for one another. May we find strength in Your love and be brave enough to follow the hidden path You have for us. Amen.

Pause

Pause for one day or one week before going to the next chapter.
>Allow the thoughts and ideas to sink in.
>Reflect.
>Ponder.
>Journal.
>Share with others.

Chapter Three

Calling

Reflection - Narooma's Lighthouse

"*In the late 1890s,*
  my great-grandmother
placed a lantern in her front window
as a humble lighthouse
for the little boats of the seaside town of Narooma,
guiding them safely home.

When storms rolled in,
and waves crashed hard against steep rocks,

The little flame would flicker,
from a kitchen window
often hidden by the rain and mist,
Yet steady as a guide to navigate
between twists and turns
across the dark abyss.

Today, the boats no longer look.
for my great-grandmother's light.
She is long gone to oceans unknown.
But something deeper has stirred us to unrest,
Boats have forgotten what to look for,
the guiding glow,
the trust,
the inner light,
of a lantern that once
welcomed strangers' home". (The author)

This reflection is based on a true story handed down through my mother's family. As a child, my mother would tell me stories about my great-grandmother, who placed a lantern in her window each night. My great-grandfather would go out fishing at night and return in the darkness before the sun had risen. When conditions were unsafe, my grandmother would remove the lantern as a signal not to enter the small harbour of Narooma, a fishing town on the south coast of New South Wales.

Across our earth, lighthouses have stood the test of time, offering safe passage through turbulent seas and away from hidden dangers such as reefs and rocks. Their light shines forth not only as a warning of dangers but also as a beacon that illuminates a path to follow. The lighthouse is often used as a metaphor for life's calling, reminding us that we do not have all the answers for the journeys we will take. Yet, in our faith and spirituality, we can often forget that light. We may no longer look for it, presuming we can navigate the paths of our lives alone. But we may experience a deeper calling, with guides and lamp posts set along the way. We can choose to seek out that light, or we can choose to ignore it. If we do, we may find ourselves crashing upon the rocks of our own making.

Who am I?

As we go through life, the answer to the question of our identity changes. As babies, we are deeply dependent on our mothers and fathers.

As a toddler, they begin to crawl and walk, testing what they can do in the wider world. Maybe Mummy or Daddy won't notice if I steal an extra cookie or biscuit? Maybe they won't notice if I run away? The child begins to develop a self-concept separate from their parent.

At age five, the child begins school, and their sense of identity becomes closely tied to friendship circles. Parents often worry tremendously about the first day of school and the days that follow. If that worry turns into anxiety, the child may absorb and reflect the parent's emotions. Like a mother bird pushing her chick out of the nest so it can learn how to fly, there is a certain goodness in what may initially seem frightening or bad.

During the teenage years, peer pressure can heavily influence who we are. Emotions bubble to the surface like volcanoes ready to explode. Teenagers often lack the emotional intelligence to identify and navigate the depth of what is going on. They may feel the emotions, but what do they truly mean? Even though teenagers express reluctance to have parents around, parents can provide a secure backdrop where the broken pieces can be swept up and held until the teenager matures.

Young adulthood presents new challenges: relationships, love, attraction, and questions of identity. During this time, we often find ourselves floating from one great idea to the next, searching for meaning. The teenage shackles no longer hold us back, and we begin to believe we are adults, or at least that we should be.

Later in life, we may realise what is more important and recognise that we won't be around forever, leading us to consider the meaning of a legacy. What do we want to leave behind? Being a grandparent, uncle, or aunt becomes a meaningful part of our identity. We have the potential to make a tremendous impact on others' lives. Our energy and wisdom can help shape the direction of not only our own families but also the wider world. We truly can make a difference. The world needs us. But the question is: are we willing to step up to the plate and play ball?

As we grow, we must recognise that our identity changes, and so too should our understanding and relationship with God. If our image of God does not mature with us or change as we grow, we risk losing touch with God altogether. God cannot remain the white-bearded figure in the sky, like a spiritual version of Santa Claus. As the mystic Meister Eckhart once wrote, *"I pray God to rid me of God"* (Rohr, Finley, & Bourgeault, 2010). Our self-concept, along with our early, childlike understanding of faith, can only take us so far. Growth requires us to go deeper, to seek a more expansive and mature relationship with the divine.

Around 1200 BCE, Moses went up Mount Sinai, he asked God, *"What is your name?"* (Exodus 3:13–14). And again, God didn't give a simple, direct answer. In Hebrew, God responds with:

"I Am Who I Am." Jews, even today, never pronounce the holy name, replacing it with silence, or some alternative such as "the Lord".

As Moses grows, we witness radical changes in his identity in the Bible. As a baby, he is a Hebrew firstborn, marked for death by Egyptian soldiers.

Paradoxically, he was raised as an Egyptian prince within the very culture that sought to destroy him. In the movie *"The Prince of Egypt"* (Chapman, Hickner, & Wells, 1998), Moses is portrayed racing horses and making reckless choices that irritate his stepbrother, Ramses. As a young adult, he discovers his truer identity as a Hebrew and, when defending a Hebrew slave, becomes embroiled in conflict. As a result, he is cast out. Having to flee into the desert, many kilometres north. He then becomes a shepherd, marries, and has children. Many years later, only then to come face to face with God and to be asked by God to return to the very place where he was thrown out.

Scholars argue whether the events in the Bible are always historically or literally true. Often, the books of the Old Testament were written centuries after the events they describe. However, as modern readers, we can interpret the meaning by asking what message or symbolism lies behind the story or Bible passage we are reading. Later in Moses' life, he became a prophet and messenger of God. Moses demands that Ramses free the Hebrew slaves, only to be rejected time and again. Ramses finally relents, but only after the death of his own young son during the final plague. As a Religious Education teacher, my students often ask, "Why did God send the angel of death to kill the firstborn?" Some Jewish and Christian scholars argue that Pharaoh's own words and actions brought judgment upon himself, making the final plague not just an act of his own decree but also a consequence of his hardened heart.

After leading the Israelites out of Egypt, Moses becomes a wanderer, an elder guiding his people through the desert. As Moses grows and changes, so does his understanding of God. Only after traveling through the desert and climbing the mountain does Moses receive God's law. The desert can serve as a metaphor for the times in our lives when we have struggled or reached a moment that has challenged us. Our deserts provide opportunities for us to grow and mature in our own faith. As we wander through our desert, our concept and understanding of God can change.

Questioning is a vital part of our journey through the desert, as it may help us to wake up. Questions allow us to deepen our understanding. As we grow and mature in faith, we must realise that this journey of our lives is not one we take alone. We grow alongside others, the people already in our lives and those we meet along the road we travel. Who we are is not defined solely by a name or by who we think we are. Who we are is shaped by the entire journey, each step along the road we call life, and each decision we make.

Mary's call

In 4 BCE, in First Century Palestine, a remote outpost of the Roman Empire, a 14-year-old girl from a small town in the northern region of Galilee was visited by an angel and called to bear a child outside of marriage. From the outside looking in, this appeared to be a pregnancy outside of wedlock. In Judaism, 2,000 years ago, this was a serious matter, as the law required stoning for such an offense. Mary was not the only one to encounter an angel. Her cousin's husband, Zechariah, also received a message from an angel, but he did not believe it.

Responding to the "call" or invitation from God can be interpreted using different perspectives. For Christians today, we can interpret the story through the lens of belief or disbelief, as well as the wider Christian tradition. However, at that time, Mary did not have the breadth of knowledge we have more than 2000 years later. The angel's invitation involved great risk. Why would God ask Mary to risk her own life? For Mary, this wasn't just about a noble idea; it was about trust to the degree of something beyond what seemed possible. It took time for the meaning of the angel's message to truly resonate and Mary, to fully understand what the call meant, until well after the event. Similarly, in our own lives, we do not recognise the pieces of the puzzle or the meaning until we have maybe taken the time to reflect and maybe chosen to step more fully into life. Responding to a call often involves stages of discovery that help us to recognise its deeper meaning. This requires courage, vulnerability, and the willingness to move beyond what seems strange.

How do we interpret a call?

We should follow Mary's example. She didn't jump to a conclusion based solely on her feelings or dismiss her experience as a hallucination. Instead, Mary pondered deeply what the angel's message might mean. She also turned to others for support, her husband and her family. Her cousin Elizabeth welcomed her, and no doubt, Mary and Elizabeth had many conversations about their meaning. Following Mary's example, discernment is not something we should do alone; it is a process that usually involves the wisdom and presence of significant people in our lives. Let us not base our decisions only on what we think individually, but on what we truly hear collectively, through prayer, reflection, and the voices of those we trust.

Lanterns and guideposts

We try to find lanterns and guideposts in our lives, someone like a spiritual guide or a compassionate counsellor, a good friend, someone who listens without judgment and is willing to walk the path with us. This doesn't mean they can provide all the answers, but rather that they can listen deeply and help us see what we may not yet recognise ourselves. Meeting regularly, whether weekly or every few weeks, can help form a meaningful spiritual companionship. In the Acts of the Apostles, Aquila and Priscilla, a husband and wife, mentored Apollos (Acts 18:24-26, NRSV). They hosted a house church and created a space for believers to gather and grow in faith. In Mark's Gospel, *"Jesus sent them out two by two and gave them authority over unclean spirits"* (Mark 6:7, NRSV). We are not meant to journey alone. We need companions who can hold us in both our highs and lows along the spiritual path.

The Ecclesiastes writer says, *"Two are better than one, because they have a good return for their labour; if either of them falls down, one can help the other up"* (4:9-10, NRSV).

CS Lewis suggested that *"friendship is born at that moment when one person says to another: 'What! You too? I thought I was the only one"* (C.S. Lewis, p61, 1960).

Furthermore, St Paul writes in the Galatians, *"carry each other's burdens, and in this way, you will fulfill the law of Christ"* (6:2, NRSV).

It seems that God has called many people to a relationship. Even when we are single, we carry within us a deep longing to connect with others, such as our wise mentors, companions or partners, trusted friends, inspiring teachers, respected community members, and family we admire. Ideally, we find spiritual lanterns and guideposts with the significant people in our lives. However, if we do not, others in the wider community may have the capacity to become our spiritual lanterns and guideposts. Do we seek them out?

A Healthy Spiritual Life

A healthy spiritual life is not just inward-focused, but outward. At different times in our lives, we are called to look beyond ourselves. Like my grandmother holding her bright lantern in the dark of night. Do we look outwardly beyond ourselves and our own concerns? This outward focus raises further questions, such as how do we serve the poor? Have we ever stopped to consider that perhaps we haven't? If we believe we've already done enough for those in need, we risk closing ourselves off from truly listening to and recognising others beyond our circle of comfort. But if we see ourselves as poor too, in need of connection, perspective, and growth, then those we serve also serve us. They can offer us a new lens through which to view the world. We can be the ones holding the lantern in the darkness, but others can also be the ones holding the lantern in our own darkness. If we try new things, like committing to feed the homeless, sitting down on the ground with homeless people, or spending time with residents in a nursing home. We are called to become who we truly are by learning from the models of those who came before us, such as Mary and other significant people in our lives who have already responded to that call. When those people are different from us, they challenge us and open us to a new perspective and a deeper vision of humanity.

God ultimately connects us to one another. When we seek communion with God by spending time pondering and reflecting and entering deep, meaningful conversations that challenge our worldview, we come into contact with Christ speaking directly to us. God is present everywhere and in all things. It is not that God needs us, but rather that we need God, for it is God who changes us through our call. We are called to become who we truly are by learning from the models of those who came before us, such as Mary and other significant people in our lives who have already responded to that call. Nurtured by spiritual lanterns and guideposts, we are led to open ourselves to creating a spiritually integrated life.

Journal

Spend 20 minutes journaling about the following.

Choose ONE of the following questions to journal about

1. *When have you experienced a sense of being called? Did it involve risk, confusion, or trust?*

2. *Who have been the spiritual lanterns or guideposts in your life, and how have they helped you to see what you may not have recognised on your own?*

3. *Are there areas in your life where there is something missing? Have you sought this out?*

4. *Have you ever encountered someone, or something, that has brought greater clarity, encouragement, or protection when you needed it?*

5. *Has the concept of God changed in the stages of your life? As you have changed, has your spirituality changed?*

Journalling

Journalling

Journalling

Journalling

Prayer

Take a moment to pause.
 Close your eyes for two to three minutes.
 Become aware of your breathing.
 Breathe slowly.
 As you breathe in and as you breathe out.
 Afterwards, if it feels helpful, consider praying slowly this prayer in the days leading up to the next chapter.

Loving God,
You call us throughout every stage of life, as a baby, toddler, child, teenager, young adult, adult, and wise elder. Help us to listen for Your voice in both the quiet and the chaos, and to recognise that our identity is not just shaped by what we do, but by who we are in You. Like Mary, may we have the courage to seek spiritual lanterns and guideposts, even when we don't understand. May we spend the time to ponder and reflect with you. Open our hearts to those who guide and walk with us. May we have the courage to search out the parts and calls that are missing from our lives. Call us beyond our comfort zones. May we go out and seek the poor both in us and around us. May we grow deeper in faith, broader in compassion for ourselves, and ever closer to the calling You invite us to. Amen.

Pause

Pause for one day or one week before going to the next chapter.

Allow the thoughts and ideas to sink in.

Reflect.

Ponder.

Journal.

Share with others.

Chapter Four

Awaken

A Reflection - Navigation

"*I had lost my bearings,*
  Turning and turning and turning.
It was only in stillness that the
spinning stopped,
I realized the alignment was off.

I was able to settle the compass.
I turned slowly,
Finding north.

Things began to be seen.
I felt more at ease when I found my
true north.

I took out my map.
I looked to the east and saw a mountain.
I looked to the south and saw a river.
I looked to the west - a tall forest.

The map of my life showed me where I was.
It wasn't easy to line up these bearings.
But there was an awakening inside me,
a realization of where I was,
and where I was called to be.

A journey with many roads and paths,
an awakening,
but more awakenings to come". (The author)

Learning to use a compass and a map when hiking in the forest or deep bushland can be challenging. Sometimes we can be tempted to take shortcuts.

When I was younger, I took a two-day hike up the Colo River, in dense forest northwest of Sydney. We had a map, a compass, and a marked path to follow. My two nephews, their friends, my brother, and I all ventured into the steep forest. I was a little silly back then, carrying an extra bag I had named "Purple," blasting Bon Jovi from a big cassette tape stereo as we walked through the bush. A few hours in, while looking at the map, we thought, "Let's cut across" to halve the time it would take to navigate the vegetation. So, we left the path that had been set before us, scrambling our way through thick forest. But we hadn't realised a cliff lay ahead. We were stuck. Still, we decided to slide down the edge, helping each other down the rocky face until we reached the river. We had arrived at a point we hadn't predicted; we were seven kilometres off course and nowhere near our planned campsite. The sun was setting. There was no path, just a river and a patch of flat grass. So, we set up camp by the river, far from where we had intended, and rested for the night.

The next morning, we tried again, aiming to cut across once more. But within a short time, we reached another cliff, this one far steeper and higher than the last. It was impossible to climb with our heavy packs. We weren't on the path. All we could see in the distance was the winding Colo River. So, we turned back. We decided to follow the twists and curves of the river, knowing it could lead us out. Eventually, we had to enter the river itself, holding our packs above our heads as water reached up to our shoulders and necks. For many kilometres, we walked through the river, still far off course. By the time we emerged, the sun was setting once again. When our families finally found us, we were late. They told us they had been about to call emergency services to send someone to search for us. We were lost. We had chosen to go off course. It was an awakening moment. Why had we gone off the path? And yet, perhaps the path we took, the one that challenged us, was the one we were meant to follow all along.

The Cost

Scott Peck's book The Road Less Travelled begins with the words, *"Life is difficult"* (p. 13, 1990). It's like trying to navigate a hike when you're lost, or when you've purposefully gone off track. Or perhaps it's like pushing a wheelbarrow full of dirt, weeds, and rocks up a steep hill. Life can feel difficult at times. It can seem meaningless, an endless cycle of adversity. Just to survive, we may already feel like we're behind the eight ball in a game of snooker or pool, as though life is designed to pull us down, as if some kind of payment always has to be made.

In ancient Jewish culture, a person was required to make sacrifices to God to atone for personal sins or the hurts they had caused. Jewish people would come to the temple in Jerusalem to offer an animal sacrifice as payment for the wrongs they had committed. Upon entry, those who were poor would purchase a small bird, while those who were more wealthy would buy a small animal, such as a lamb. The Jewish priest would whisper the person's sins into the ear of the animal before it was slaughtered. This practice of animal sacrifice ceased with the destruction of the Jewish temple in 70 AD.

Even after death, ancient religions recognised the concept of cost and payment. In Greek mythology, it was believed that souls had to cross the River Styx to enter the underworld, and a coin was placed in the mouth of the deceased to pay the ferryman who would carry them across. Whilst in ancient Egyptian religion, the journey to the afterlife required passing through various trials and overcoming obstacles, such as the Lake of Fire. In Mesopotamian culture, the underworld was difficult to access, and one had to pass through seven gates to reach it.

But the idea of "cost" is also found in science. In biology, apoptosis is the intentional destruction of cells to prevent overgrowth and disease. Apoptosis removes unnecessary or damaged cells, helping to prevent conditions like cancer by eliminating cells with genetic damage. Scientists now recognize that short intermittent fasting is a powerful way to stimulate apoptosis and restore balance by triggering the body's natural cellular cleanup process.

In physics, Albert Einstein's understanding of the Second Law of Thermodynamics states that entropy, the measure of disorder in a system, will always increase over time in a closed system. This supports the idea that systems, including biological ones, naturally break down and decline over time. Einstein recognized that there was a certain order to the universe, suggesting a reason or purpose behind how things are. He once stated, *"Science without religion is lame; religion without science is blind"* (Einstein, p. 46, 1941).

Like a clock that slowly winds down with each passing moment, marking time with the steady tick of its hands, its energy gradually fades until a master hand steps in to wind it back up. This winding brings the springs and gears back to life, setting everything in motion once again.

Why is it that across the world, in all ancient cultures, there is a shared need to recognize an outside force that sets things in motion? It seems that, deep within the human experience, within the cycles of life, death, and decay, there is an innate awareness that there must be something more. Not just the ego's desire for recognition beyond this life, but a sense that something existed before we did. Not just our grandfathers and great-grandmothers, but something far older, something that set the universe in motion. The very design and order of the universe suggest the existence of a first cause, pointing to a divine origin.

Christians, like believers of many religions, believe that this first cause is God. Christians go further, saying God entered creation in human form. They call this the Incarnation. God not only created the universe, but also chose to step into it. But why? The Franciscan friar Richard Rohr asks the question, *"Was it to meet some sort of cosmic payment system for the sins of the world? Why would God need to pay God self?"*(Rohr, Finley, & Bourgeault, 2010) That doesn't seem to make sense. No, Christians believe that God entered creation out of love.

It seems that there is no situation in which God waves a magic wand and instantly fixes everything. God doesn't come to us as a distant memory but is woven into the very fabric of our lives. It is through our vulnerability that God reveals Himself. In the very act of winding down and falling apart, God begins the work of winding things back up. Jesus says, *"If anyone would come after me, let them deny themselves and follow me"* (Luke 14:27, NRSV). Pope Benedict comments that, *"the world offers you comfort, but you were not made for comfort. You were made for greatness"* (2005). And as Scripture reminds us, *"We must go through many hardships to enter the Kingdom of God"* (Acts 14:22).

But it is not just we who have to pay the cost. We stand on the shoulders of giants, not only those who came before us, but on the foundation of what God has done and continues to do through us and the people who have come before us. The cost of discipleship is not ours alone to bear. There is a cost that others carry now, and others have carried before us. One that Jesus Himself bore. We do not stand alone. God stands with us. In the midst of things falling apart, God reaches out and says, *"Take my hand"* (Matthew 14:31, NRSV), just as Jesus did when Peter began to drown.

At the Last Supper, Jesus says, *"Take and eat, this is my body"* (Matthew 26:26). He gives us His very self. This is not merely a theory or a nice idea in our minds. To enter into the Christian life is to have a real, physical encounter with the person of Jesus Christ. In our lives, we are called to reflect the divine spark within us. At the end of John's Gospel, Jesus breathes on His disciples and says, *"Receive the Holy Spirit"* (John 20:22). This is not just our own spirit at work; it is God's Spirit, living and moving in us.

Bethany Hamilton once said, *"It is hard to see the bigger picture when you are caught up in the storm, but I believe that God gives us strength to get through anything"* (McNamara, 2011). Bethany lost her arm after a shark attack while surfing, an experience that caused her to lose sight of God for a time. Pain and suffering often take centre stage in our lives. It's only later, when we step back and reflect on the bigger picture, that we might begin to see how God has been active in our lives all along.

Stages of Awakening

As we grow through life, we may experience different stages of awakening. Like a seedling placed in a small punnet, we may start small, but we soon outgrow our original space. The gardener then replants the seedling into a larger pot, adding fresh soil and fertilizer. Each time the plant is moved, it experiences shock, a disruption in its environment. The same is true for us. When we are called to change our circumstances, we are also called to grow. As children, we transition from home to preschool, and eventually to school. As adults, we might change careers, enter or leave relationships, or even move to an entirely new country. Each change requires us to re-learn how things work, and naturally, there is a degree of shock and resistance that comes with these transitions. Hopefully, this shock is big enough to shatter our old way of being, so that we open our hearts to enter the new.

Liminal Space

Richard Rohr says that one of the only ways to truly wake up is through liminal space (p. 135-139, 2005). Liminal spaces are those transitional periods in our lives when we move from one way of being to another. These are times when we are no longer in control and cannot fully see what lies ahead, which often causes stress and uncertainty. Rohr suggests that we do not have the willpower alone to bring about deep transformation. Instead, liminal space presents us with something so powerful that it can shatter our ego script and ways of seeing, prompting us to re-evaluate our assumptions about life. Liminal spaces can affect us psychologically, spiritually, cognitively, emotionally, and physically. It's like standing between two worlds: we have left the old behind but have not yet fully arrived in the new. When we leave school, the years that follow can be deeply transitional, as young adults begin exploring who they are and how the world works, often accompanied by uncertainty and discomfort that might make them want to run away. Liminal spaces challenge and sometimes force, us to step out of our comfort zones. However, we can also consciously enter liminal spaces, such as when we volunteer to care for the poor, go on a mission trip, or immerse ourselves in another culture. Experiencing a radically different culture or encountering deep poverty can awaken us to a new way of living in the world.

Liminal spaces offer great potential for growth. They provide us with new perspectives and, if we are open to the experience, can reshape how we view reality. However, these transitional spaces can also appear unexpectedly. When someone close to us dies or becomes seriously ill, it can shatter the pattern or script of how we can presume the world works. Such events often lead us to ask deeper questions about life and why suffering occurs. In these moments, we may seek wisdom from a higher or more experienced source, which can help deepen our awakening. We gain insight and maturity through the struggles we endure, as we learn to see life differently. At the same time, trauma can also cause us to regress, mentally, emotionally, or spiritually, making us feel as though the clock of our lives is not winding forward, but winding backward.

There is a disruption of normalcy when the regular ways of doing things no longer work. Divorce or the breakdown of relationships can shatter the familiar patterns of our lives. We may no longer be able to depend on loved ones as we once did. This can require us to change, taking on either more or less responsibility than before. Living with someone who has dementia or Alzheimer's, for example, presents a heartbreaking shift. The film *"The Notebook"* (Cassavetes, 2004) beautifully portrays the deep love Noah has for his wife, Allie. Despite the strength of their lifelong bond, it cannot save her from the devastating effects of dementia. Noah's heart breaks as he slowly loses the woman he loves. Allie no longer sees Noah as her beloved but as someone who threatens her, a stranger. Though Noah still loves her deeply, this emotional toll is unbearable for many. These liminal spaces can stretch on for long periods, leading us to lose hope. Yet maybe hope is not found in a miracle cure or a return to what was. Maybe true hope is the willingness to remain present and faithful in the darkness of our lives.

Liminal spaces can be understood as sacred thresholds or holy ground (Rohr, p. 47-52, 2003) where our old ways of seeing no longer serve us, and something deeper begins to unfold. These moments invite us to step more fully into the raw truth of our lives, where the surface gives way to the sacred. In entering this space we begin to notice that God is not absent, but often hidden in the ordinary fabric of our experiences, subtly woven through moments of uncertainty and loss. It is here, in the stillness between what was and what is becoming, that we can attune ourselves to a presence greater than our own. These sacred pauses do not leave us unchanged. They mark a turning point, a crossing from one way of being into another. And in that crossing, like a river, we awaken to a new world, and a new self, shaped not by control or certainty, but by something else.

In the story of the Road to Emmaus in Luke's Gospel (24:13-35), we encounter a profound moment of transformation for two disciples. This story unfolds after the crucifixion and death of Jesus in 30AD Palestine. Two followers are walking along the road, trying to piece together the puzzle of recent events. They are moving away from Jerusalem, discussing the shocking and heartbreaking things that have happened to their friend Jesus. Confused and uncertain, both because of their fear of the Romans and the rumours they've heard about Jesus being alive, they struggle to make sense of it all. As they walk, Jesus Himself appears and begins to journey with them, though they do not recognize Him. Strangely, they fail to identify Him, perhaps because He has changed in some way. But rather than revealing His identity right away, Jesus invites them into deeper reflection. He doesn't say, "Hey guys, it's me, Jesus." Instead, He allows them to remain in their liminal space, a place of questioning and searching. He guides them through the Scriptures, encouraging understanding to unfold gradually. It is only later, in the breaking of the bread, that their eyes are opened, and they finally recognize Him. They are deeply moved, exclaiming, *"Were not our hearts burning within us while He talked with us on the road?"* (Luke 24:32, NRSV) Their hearts recognized the truth long before their minds caught up, reminding us that spiritual insight often begins with the heart and body.

The Emmaus story teaches us how we are called to wake up to a deeper awareness. We are invited to step into situations that feel uncomfortable, not to immediately fix or solve them, but to discover a new reality we may not yet recognise. Questioning is a critical part of awakening. It allows us to deepen our understanding. But this understanding is not just an intellectual exercise; it involves our whole being, our minds, our bodies, and our hearts. Often, our hearts perceive truth before our minds, which may be clouded by the emotions we experience. It's important to recognise that we rarely go through these transitions alone. Even in times when we feel isolated, we often journey through liminal spaces alongside others, the people already in our lives and those we meet along the road of life.

Waking up is not simply a choice we make, but something that often happens to us as life unfolds. As we journey through various seasons, we encounter liminal moments, times of transition, uncertainty, and even darkness that quietly shape and transform us. These spaces may feel disorienting or painful, yet they hold the potential for deep awakening. One day, often when looking back, we come to realise that what once seemed like darkness was, in fact, the hidden path toward light, a sacred invitation to a call that had remained hidden as we lived our lives.

Journal

Spend 20 minutes journaling about the following.

Choose ONE of the following questions to journal about

1. What moments in your life have felt like things were falling apart or winding down?

2. How do you respond to liminal spaces, those uncertain or transitional times in life when your usual ways of thinking or living no longer work?

3. Have you ever experienced a time of suffering or confusion that later led to personal growth, clarity, or a deeper connection with God?

4. The chapter suggests that God's presence is often hidden within the ordinary and the painful. Where in your own life might God be quietly at work right now?

5. What does "the cost of discipleship" mean to you, and how have others' sacrifices (including those of Jesus) shaped your journey of faith?

6. Like the disciples on the road to Emmaus, when have your heart and emotions recognised a spiritual truth before your mind did?

7. How are you being invited to "wake up" right now, to move from comfort to courage, from control to trust, or from shallowness to depth?

Journalling

Journalling

Journalling

Journalling

Prayer

Take a moment to pause.
 Close your eyes for two to three minutes.
 Become aware of your breathing.
 Breathe slowly.
 As you breathe in and as you breathe out.
 Afterwards, if it feels helpful, consider praying slowly this prayer in the days leading up to the next chapter.

Loving and faithful God,
In the midst of our struggles, uncertainties, and liminal spaces, awaken to go on the journey of faith. When life winds down and feels dark, help us trust that You are quietly at work, winding us back up, shaping us through love, not force. Give us the courage to embrace the cost of following You, to walk through the storms with hope, and to recognise You, like the disciples on the road to Emmaus, not always in clarity, but in broken bread, in quiet moments, and in the burning of our hearts. May we awaken to the sacred hidden in the ordinary, and find the light that was always waiting in the dark. Amen.

Pause

Pause for one day or one week before going to the next chapter.
    Allow the thoughts and ideas to sink in.
    Reflect.
    Ponder.
    Journal.
    Share with others.

Chapter Five

Igniting justice

A Reflection - Red and Yellow Flags

"The sun rose again on a hot summer's day.
    Many headed to the beach to escape the sun's rays.
A thousand people parking their families on the hot sand,
Towels, eskies, and beach umbrellas.
Sea birds hovered above, ready to swoop down.

Earlier in the morning, the red and yellow flags stood tall.
Lifeguards stood nearby
With a paddleboard, a jet ski, and a flotation device,

Waiting for tourists who didn't know
Where to stand:
Between the flags.

The swell was up.
Waves crashed down.
A hidden rip in the dark water
Waited to pull swimmers out to sea, to drown.

Fun had been the motivation for coming to the sand.
The coolness invited us to jump in.
But in an instant, when Mum and Dad weren't watching,
The child was swept out to sea.
Moving and moving and moving.
Above the water. Below the water.
Above the water. Below the water.

The child's life flashed before their eyes.
Thinking, would they survive?

Then a hand reached down,
Just like Jesus pulled Peter up,
The red and yellow lifesavers
reached for the child's hand.
They saw, even before they knew,
What was coming?
The child needed help.
The child didn't want to drown.

The jet ski took them back to land.
Family waiting
With eyes full of tears and stress.
Mum reached down, hugging their small child.
"What were you doing?"
"Playing," the child responded.

And all the parents could do was give thanks.
To the people guarding
Between the red and yellow flags".
(The author)

In Australia, lifeguards play a critical role in preventing drownings. Each day at the beach and in the ocean, water conditions can change rapidly, from a calm, fun-filled environment to a life-threatening situation where lives are at risk. Unaware of how to read the wave conditions, many people fail to navigate these dangers. The role of lifeguards goes to the heart of what justice is about. In life, there are certain things that should happen, such as saving a human life, and certain values that must be protected, such as treating people with dignity and respect. Social justice seeks to reach the heart of injustice, wherever it may be found among refugees, the homeless, victims of domestic violence, and those suffering from the impacts of climate change. But do we really care? Are these injustices truly our concern?

A short story

George was a man who liked to sit on the couch on a Friday night. Betty, George's friend from university days, invited him to volunteer with the

St Vincent de Paul food van that Friday. George replied, "Thank you for the invitation, but I have an important appointment on Friday." In truth, George mistrusted why homeless people needed food handouts, thinking that they should simply get a job. By Friday, he felt quite exhausted from work, and the last thing he wanted was to drive aimlessly around the city, talking to random homeless people. George enjoyed his TV time on Friday night, and nothing, not even Betty, his friend, was going to change his mind.

Business as usual

Each of us can act like George. At different points in life, especially when we are very busy and life seems demanding, people lack the will or capacity to act against injustice. Justice calls us to challenge our ego-driven agendas, to get off the couch. Sometimes culture reinforces our own comfortable mindsets through entertainment and the pursuit of wealth, so doing what Betty proposed may go against our desire to do what we want. However, as Christians, we are called not only to empathise with those who suffer, but to give of our very being, and that takes something from us, our own agendas. We can become caught in the endless loop of "business as usual" and miss the short window to make a difference.

The poor as a doorway

In the film The Pursuit of Happyness (Muccino, 2006), Will Smith plays Chris Gardner, a father who struggles with his relationships and finances. His wife, Linda, leaves him due to unfulfilled promises, such as not paying bills and failing to fulfill commitments to their son. Chris's dream of becoming a stockbroker leads him down a path with no steady income. He tries to run a business selling bone density scanners to doctors, but the doctors often cannot afford them. Gradually, he loses everything:

his house, his car, and his marriage. In the grip of poverty, Chris is forced to sleep in a train station bathroom with his young son. Even this refuge is threatened when, late at night at 2 am, a cleaner attempts to enter and remove them. Chris loses everything, security and dignity in a home, to provide for his son, as the cleaner bangs at the toilet door in the dead of night. Chris hits rock bottom.

In the Old Testament, God comes to liberate those who are suffering and is often seen on the side of the poor. The poor in the Old Testament, such as refugees, widows, foreigners, and orphans. People like Chris, who have nothing and who suffer the most. Despite their hardships, the Bible shows these people often placing their trust in God. The Psalmist declares, *"The meek will inherit the earth"* (Psalm 37:11, NRSV) and *"God arose to judgment to save all the humble of the earth"* (Psalm 76:9, NRSV). In Deuteronomy, it says: *"But the Egyptians mistreated us, afflicted us, and laid hard labour upon us. Then we cried to the Lord, the God of our fathers, and the Lord heard our voice and saw our affliction"* (Deuteronomy 26:6 7, NRSV). God often sent prophets to liberate the poor and to speak out against injustice. The prophet Isaiah writes, *"The Spirit of the Lord is upon me, because the Lord has anointed me to bring good news to the poor"* (61:1, NRSV). This is the same reading Jesus proclaims at the beginning of his ministry.

God chose not to stand at a distance and help but chose to enter the reality of what it is like to be poor in the person of Jesus Christ. God acts on behalf of the poor. Saint Paul writing to the Philippians says, *"Though he was in the form of God, he did not consider equality with God something to be grasped. Instead, he emptied himself, taking the form of a servant, being born in human likeness"* (2:6-7). Further in the Gospel of Mark, *"For the Son of Man did not come to be served, but to serve and to give his life as a ransom for many"* (10:45). God pours out His Spirit and becomes what it is like to be poor. God entered the world as a fragile baby, and he became poor. Whilst, as an adult, Jesus sought out the poor, using his energy and will to serve them.

God is always working out of love. This is not just an emotion, but a love that acts. God's desire is to express love through life. Suffering is not something we are called to pursue for its own sake; rather, it is often the by-product of what God is doing or maybe we are doing, but this love seeks to lift up the lowly and overcome death itself. Death on a cross. Jesus became one with us in suffering, but it is precisely in this moment, when life falls apart, that God acts. God's Spirit is seen more clearly in poverty than in wealth. It is when stripped of dignity and when the ego is emptied that God acts.

Again, in the film The Pursuit of Happyness, it is precisely when Chris Gardner accepts his situation, desperate to find refuge in the train station, that things begin to change. Sitting on a train station bench with his son, in the midst of their fragile circumstances, Chris uses his imagination to transform the situation. During the day, Chris pretends that his bone density scanner, which he is trying to sell to doctors for an exorbitant price, is actually a time machine. He turns the dial, and he and his son travel back in time to the age of the dinosaurs. Through the power of imagination, Chris enters the world with his son, and together they are better able to cope with their reality, to sleep rough in a public toilet. In their minds, they find a cave where they hide from ferocious dinosaurs.

Brueggemann (1978) argues that the Spirit-inspired prophetic imagination enables believers to envision an alternative world of hope and justice (p. 13, 40-41). Mark Patrick Hederman, a Benedictine monk, in his book The Opal and the Pearl and the Haunted Inkwell, suggests that the Holy Spirit moves through imagination, offering a new way of seeing the world (2008). Hederman describes the Holy Spirit as constantly nudging humanity toward transformation, helping people break free from rigid, overly rational ways of thinking. He suggests that the Holy Spirit works through prayerful imagination, in which contemplation and creativity merge to foster a deeper relationship with God. God desires to shatter the parts of us that prevent us from experiencing divine love or to break the bonds of oppression in the world so as to dismantle the limited perspectives that hinder us from fully participating in God's vision for all of creation.

Jesus also uses imagination. He teaches through parables, inviting people to envision a new way of seeing the world.

"Listen! A sower went out to sow.

And as he sowed, some seeds fell on the path, and the birds came and ate them up.

Other seeds fell on rocky ground, where they had little soil, and sprang up quickly because they had no depth of soil.

But when the sun rose, they were scorched; and since they had no root, they withered away.

Other seeds fell among thorns, and the thorns grew up and choked them.

Other seeds fell on good soil and brought forth grain, some a hundredfold, some sixty, some thirty.

Let anyone with ears listen!" (Matthew 13:3-9)

Jesus's parable speaks to a largely rural, peasant society. The people he speaks to would be familiar with the language and concepts he uses. We can interpret the "seed" as our faith, but we can see that many of his parables can be applied to social injustice. Do we respond to people in need when the invitation is given? What fruit do we bear when we are asked to respond to those in need?

In the Beatitudes, Jesus states, *"Blessed are the poor"* (in Luke's Gospel) and *"Blessed are the poor in spirit"* (in Matthew's Gospel). Our minds race with the question, "How can this be true?" We often resist letting go of our riches and our comfort. Yet God is not declaring that wealth or riches are inherently bad; rather, they are to be used not for our own sakes, but for lifting up the poor. The followers of Jesus are called to play an active role in God's kingdom. Where our riches are given away, for example *"the woman with an alabaster jar of very expensive perfume, made of pure nard. She broke the jar and poured the perfume on Jesus' head"* (Mark 14:3-9, NRSV). Out of love, she acts to give Jesus a sense of dignity and worth. Some of Jesus' own disciples do not understand what she is doing. Often, our attachment to wealth prevents us from fully experiencing God's vision for our lives. This can be equally applied to other aspects of our lives, such as our time and our willingness to care for the poor. It is only when we empty ourselves, like the woman, that God's Spirit can dwell more deeply within us. Just as God emptied Himself, so too are we invited to do the same.

Are we willing to empty ourselves? Do we set our hearts on the valleys and roadblocks of our lives or do we look for something more? Do we focus on our possessions and wealth? God's love moves beyond the valleys and possessions we experience in life. When we experience poverty and emptiness, a path opens that can lead us toward freedom from what holds us back. We can be humbled and transformed by what God is doing in our lives. When gold is dug from the earth, it contains some impurities such as rock and other metals. The gold must pass through fire to be refined into something that contains purer gold. This gold is a metaphor for our own inner transformation, a symbol of awakening when we step towards the places of injustice in our lives.

In Japanese culture, the "art of kintsugi" restores broken ceramic pots by mending their cracks with gold. Instead of hiding the brokenness, kintsugi highlights the fractures, celebrating their history and making the object more valuable. Japanese artists carefully take the broken pieces and slowly work out how they fit together. The gold allows the broken pottery pieces to join back together. Kintsugi is a powerful metaphor, as it shows that our brokenness and cracks can reveal the great beauty and value of who we are. The golden outline in the pot restores wholeness, but never forgets the broken pieces that were once split apart. The brokenness and fractures become a gift to something more. A hidden treasure.

Similarly, Jesus washes the disciples' feet as an act of service, an expression of his love. He models what they are called to do, but more importantly, he provides them with a sense of intrinsic dignity. Each of them reflects the goodness and beauty of God. The washing of the feet reminds them, and us, that we, too, have deep value. Especially in moments that seem dirty, like the disciples' feet, or broken, like a Japanese clay pot. In broader life, we are called to seek out moments of injustice and see them as doorways to restore dignity that may have been lost. We are called to recognise the needs of the poor, not only the financially or spiritually poor, but also those parts within ourselves that have fallen short of becoming fully alive. Alive with the possibility of God's love and hope.

To say to the broken, "You are my brother," or "You are my sister," is to affirm and recognise that "you are a child of God." Our gift to others is a reminder of their immeasurable dignity. This does not mean ignoring brokenness or trying to magically fix it, but instead, seeing in it the place where God's light shines through, not as guilt or shame, but as goodness. We are like the Kintsugi pot with the broken cracks. Where our broken pieces and fractures once were, gold can be used to bring them together, making us more whole. What is this gold in our lives? We must discover for ourselves what this gold is at a deeper level.

A heart response

When we see the suffering or plight of someone face-to-face. Especially those people or things we deeply care about, there is something within us that compels us to change. To move beyond what we normally do, and to act in a way that seeks to act against injustice. We can talk about statistics like forty percent of women and girls who have experienced domestic violence, or that more than 110,000 sleep rough each night, or that in 2021, there were 51 million slaves worldwide. But it is not until we make things personal, personal in our own lives, that things begin to change. Do we get off the couch? Do we look in the eyes of another human being and recognise the sufferings they face?

As Nick Brown, a Street Retreat[1] guide and youth leader in Sydney, suggests, *"we need to develop eyes of compassion"*, which he attributes to his pastor Ken. On Street Retreat, participants sometimes sit on the ground in a circle with a homeless person, show genuine interest by asking questions, and actively listen to their story. This process may become a bridge between who each participant is and who the other is. The power of someone's

---

1. Street Retreat is a social justice program which takes 15 students for an entire weekday walking the streets of Sydney meeting homeless people and learning about various homeless services. The power of listening to the story of a homeless people allows participants to gain a deep sense of what it means to be homeless. Nick Brown is the program leader and guide who is available for school, church or small groups.

story, especially when shared openly and authentically, can open each person up to a new way of being in the world. Suffering caused by injustice can seem overwhelming. Our sufferings connect us and remind us that we all suffer. When we see poverty in others, we may become more open to recognising it in ourselves. It's as if the wounds of Christ publicly flow like blood and water from the cross, wounds with the power to transform. Not just Christ's wounds, but also our own, and those of the people around us.

Vinnies

Organisations like St Vincent de Paul[2] or the Baptist ministry Hope Street [3] in Sydney call each of us to make a difference.

In my early 20s, I was like George. A friend introduced me to the St Vincent de Paul food van, which prepared sandwiches in a small kitchen near Parramatta in Sydney and then drove west to Penrith train station, about 30 minutes away. I started getting off the couch on Friday nights to feed the homeless, all because of a friend's invitation. We didn't go alone; we went as part of a team. I was nervous, and something inside me resisted

---

2. St Vincent De Paul is a Catholic welfare organisation which provides a range of services that help the poor. These services may include a men's drop-in centre like Matthew Talbot in Sydney or the Vinnies Food Van which goes out on the streets of Sydney to feed the homeless.

3. Hope Street is a Baptist Church ministry based in Woolloomooloo, near Kings Cross in Sydney, that offers a range of vital support services to the local community. The ministry operates a café, an op shop, a youth afternoon centre, and a variety of social programs designed to assist those in need. With a particular focus on supporting the homeless and vulnerable.

stepping out. I felt fear. Yet at the same time, there was a desire to make a difference and to spend time with my friend. Inside me was a tension, like a seesaw in a children's park or a tug-of-war, between wanting to go and wanting to stay.

At Penrith train station, I stood behind a white table filled with food and drinks. That table felt like a barrier between me and those we were there to serve. Meanwhile, my friend would walk around and sit in the gutter about ten metres away, chatting and laughing with many of the street people, mostly teenagers, who had come out for a hot chocolate and a freshly made peanut butter sandwich. I may have been sharing food and drink, but my friend was sharing her presence, laughter, and curiosity. It reminded me of the story of Mary and Martha (Luke 10:38-42), I was Martha, busy serving, and my friend was Mary, sitting at Jesus' feet, listening to the homeless people.

As the night came to a close and we drove the van back to the St. Vincent de Paul kitchen, a euphoric feeling filled the air. We might never meet those people again, but for a brief moment, through action, we had become a family, a community that cared for one another.

But sometimes, it takes a major event to wake us up to the injustices in the world. From September 2019, massive fires started to devastate the east coast of Australia. These fires were so severe that they continued to burn into January, five months later. Despite extensive bushfire firefighting resources, including water-bombing aircraft, the fires could not be contained. Sydney was engulfed in a thick soup of dark smoke, and asthmatics were warned not to go outside. The fires stretched for more than 1,000 kilometres, from Victoria to northern New South Wales. Afterwards, researchers estimated that more than half a billion animals had died in a short time, including koalas, kangaroos, possums, lizards, birds, and wallabies. Amidst all this devastation, people began to respond with generosity. Members of the Sikh and Muslim communities drove vans to remote areas affected by the fires, offering freshly cooked meals. It was as though something deep within people had awakened. Witnessing the loss of life, homes, and the heavy sadness in people's hearts stirred a deeper need to act. Our shared humanity called us to care and to step out of our comfort zones. Amid the devastation, some hearts were changed.

Today, do we only care for one another in a time of crisis? Have we forgotten the call to love the other? Jesus' great commandment of love (Matthew 22:37–39) can be diverted amid a thousand activities that pull our attention away. What do we do when we have fallen out of love? When couples make their vows, they promise to care for each other "in sickness and in health." Yet little do they realise that it is in the struggles and difficulties of life where love most truly appears. Love is most fully expressed in moments marked by the absence of love.

"Bastille" is an emotional segment from the 2006 anthology film *"Paris, Je T'aime" (Payne, 2006)*. Set in the 12th arrondissement of Paris, the story follows a middle-aged man named Jean-Marc, who has grown bored and emotionally distant in his marriage. He's planning to leave his wife, Fanny, for a younger woman with whom he's been having an affair. He rehearses how he'll break the news to Fanny, his wife, preparing himself for freedom and a new life. He sets a lunch date with his wife and prepares to tell her the bad news. During lunch, everything soon changes when Fanny initially hands her husband a letter revealing to him that she is dying of leukemia. At that moment, Jean-Marc faces an emotional choice. Instead of following through with his plan to tell his wife he will leave for a young woman, he chooses to stay. Something awakens within Jean-Marc to care for his loving wife, who is dying. In the weeks and months that follow, Jean-Marc cares for his wife, cooking, cleaning, comforting. He is reminded of the love that ignited their marriage. Jean-Marc dresses differently, listens to her, and tries

to make her laugh. He begins seeing her again, not as a routine or a burden, but as someone worthy of love and joy. Through these loving actions, he falls back into love with his wife. Not out of guilt or obligation, but the absence of something he is about to lose. He even says that he "fell in love with her again, like the first time." His transformation is subtle, but sincere. This is a justice of the heart where Jean-Marc makes a conscious decision to honour his vows, to see his wife, and to give her the dignity of being loved as she prepares to die. In doing so, Jean-Marc becomes a man who loves not out of selfish desire, but one who is willing to sacrifice himself. Scott Peck (p. 85-88, 1990) describes love as when you extend yourself for the betterment of the other.

Love can change people's hearts. We see this also in the film The Mission (Joffé, 1986), set in the 1700s in South America. Rodrigo Mendoza, a former mercenary and slave trader, undergoes a profound personal conversion. After killing his own brother in a fit of rage, Mendoza falls into dark despair. Fortunately, he is offered a chance at redemption when Jesuit missionary Father Gabriel invites him to live among the native Guarani people, the very people Mendoza had recently tried to enslave. In a key scene, Mendoza carries a heavy bundle of armour on his own back up a steep waterfall and cliff. The armour symbolizes his guilt and shame. As he climbs, he begins to falter. Just when it seems he may fall and die below the cliff, a Guarani tribesman, the Guarani he once tried to enslave, cuts the rope tying Mendoza to the armour, sending the metal bundle crashing down the cliff. Freed from the weight, Mendoza experiences a flood of emotion, a merciful embrace of love and forgiveness. This loving act from the Guarani man restores Mendoza's hope and changes his heart.

We, too, need to experience this kind of love, especially when we have lost all hope, the love of God, through the love of another person. This love is not meant to be kept for ourselves, but given away. When we encounter true love, it has the power to transform us from within. Are we willing to love someone we do not love? Are we willing to open our hearts to the love of the other?

True justice is love in action. When love is absent, a force must rise strong enough to break through the void; that force is mercy. Mercy is unexpected love. We are called to be channels through which this love can be realized and made visible in the world. Do we call upon this love in our own lives? Have we recognised that the essence of love is caring for one another? Are we willing to let love in to shape who we are? Are we willing to participate in the creative work of love? Love that acts in faith and seeks hope.

Journal

Spend 20 minutes journaling about the following.

Choose ONE of the following questions to journal about

1. *When have you been given an invitation to respond to injustice?*

2. *When have you found yourself, like George, resisting an opportunity to serve others? What held you back, and what might help you to say "yes" next time?*

3. *What "armour" or burdens of guilt, pride, or fear do you carry that need to be let go so you can more freely live out love and justice?*

4. *In what ways have you experienced moments when loss, suffering, or hardship led to deeper compassion?*

5. *Jesus used imagination through parables. How might imagination help you see the world and justice from a new perspective?*

6. *Are there parts of your life, like the broken pottery in the art of kintsugi, where your wounds could become sources of beauty and connection for others?*

Journalling

Journalling

Journalling

Journalling

Prayer

Take a moment to pause.
   Close your eyes for two to three minutes.
   Become aware of your breathing.
   Breathe slowly.
   As you breathe in and as you breathe out.
   Afterwards, if it feels helpful, consider praying slowly this prayer in the days leading up to the next chapter.

Loving and merciful God,
You who walk with the poor, the broken, and the forgotten, open our eyes to see the world as You see it. Help us to empty ourselves of pride and fear so that Your Spirit may dwell deeply within us. May our broken pieces be restored by your hope living in us and those around us. Teach us to have eyes of compassion that move beyond our judgments and look into the eyes of the human person. Call us to care for those in need. May we be channels and instruments of Your unexpected mercy. Enable us to transform dark places so that love may restore what has been lost. Change our hearts, Lord, so that in loving others, we may be drawn ever closer to You. Amen.

Pause

Pause for one day or one week before going to the next chapter.

Allow the thoughts and ideas to sink in.

Reflect.

Ponder.

Journal.

Share with others.

Chapter Six

Love in sacrifice

A Reflection - Love is blind

"When I was seven, I ran through the yard,
　　Playing kiss and catch, my heart beating hard.
Brown eyes, brown hair, a girl full of grace,
I found "love" in her smile, her chase.
And I thought: what real love is.

At fourteen, waiting for my train,
A stranger stared and sparked a flame.
I hoped she'd come again the next day,

But silence met the tracks that lay.
And I thought: what real love is.

Eighteen came with dreams held tight:
Fast cars, bright lights, and riches in sight.
A pretty face, a life well-fed,
But love felt shallow in my head.
And I thought: what real love is.

At twenty, letters filled with rhyme,
Words of longing, stitched through time.
Speaking of life, of soul, of skies,
Of questions that poetry never denies.
And I thought: what real love is.

At twenty-four, my spirit stirred,
A monk's life called with sacred word.
Community, prayer, and service run deep,
Yet love still roused me from my sleep.
So, I dated, and still I sought,
Still, I thought: what real love is.

At thirty, vows beneath the sun,
A life with another had begun.
Through sickness, health, joy, and strain,
Through children's laughter and parents' pain,
Through meals and lawns and midnight cries,
Through every no and each goodbye,
I thought: what real love is.

Now greying slightly, lines on my face,
Time has slowed my hurried pace.
And I wonder still, with gentle grace:
Love is not just found in a warm embrace,
Not just passion, not just kiss,
But presence, truth, and quiet bliss.

Love is more than just a spark or tear,
Love is not a feeling; it is who we are here.
I thought: What real love is". (The author)

Understanding and the depth of love are lifelong. The experience of human love invites us to reflect beyond. Love stirs in us and awakens in us to care for others. Love is not just an emotion. The Greeks had several words for love, such as "Filos" or friendship love, "Eros" or erotic love, and "Agape" or a love which serves. Yet, in English, we only have one word. Are we missing something? Do we not realise that when we love someone, we are called to engage the many aspects of what love is?

Dorothy Day

Dorothy Day grew up in the early 1920s as an American journalist and social activist. As a young woman, she had several romantic relationships (Ellsberg, 1992). Her first was a passionate love affair with the American journalist Lionel Moise. Lionel had no interest in religion and held strongly left-wing views. When Dorothy became pregnant, Lionel pressured her into having an abortion, as he did not want to be a father. This experience led Dorothy into a deep depression, a deep sadness, and darkness surrounded her, and left her with lasting emotional scars.

Later, she entered a new relationship with biologist Forster Batterham. They shared a deep love for nature, literature, and the cause of social justice. They lived together in a committed but unmarried relationship, reflecting their shared beliefs in freedom and personal autonomy. When Dorothy became pregnant a second time, she refused to abort the child, despite Forster's initial reluctance. Carrying her baby daughter, something deep inside Dorothy stirred: a sense of gratitude and awe. Dorothy found something new. Tamar was born.

As the months and years passed, Dorothy discovered a profound sense of love through her motherhood. The experience brought new meaning to her life and opened her heart to God. Her relationship with her daughter changed how she viewed the world, revealing beauty in everyday moments. Despite Forster's opposition, Dorothy began attending church. Maternal love had changed her heart, making it something beyond herself. Deep love can make us vulnerable like children; it can draw us into others' lives. Children can help us to step outside our world and walk in their vulnerability; we begin to see things differently. We can begin to look beyond the barriers and roadblocks that we have created.

Parents are often called to make great sacrifices for their children. They must think not only of themselves or their partners, but of the needs and well-being of their children. It can be difficult for parents to let go of the routines of work and entertainment, and instead, place a fragile baby at the centre of who they are. The psychologist Carl Rogers once wrote, *"We cannot move away from what we are, until we thoroughly accept what we are"* (Rogers, p. 17, 1961). Raising our children, or others' children, helps us to know ourselves better, which may lead to a deeper acceptance of ourselves. However, our human blind spots sometimes prevent us from fully loving as we are called to. For many parents, it is difficult to shift their sense of self from that of individuals, colleagues, or businesspeople to that of caregivers.

Yet it is often through the struggles we experience as parents or caregivers that we can help reflect on the deeper realities.

Parenting can be quite challenging. The sacrifices parents make often call them to go beyond the simple bonds of blood. True sacrifice invites us to love more deeply and selflessly. Consider, for example, the inspiring story of Moira Kelly.

Moira Kelly

One morning in 1998, Australian humanitarian Moira Kelly boarded a plane bound for war-torn Iraq (60 Minutes Australia, 2011). There, she found Emmanuel, a small child abandoned in an orphanage. Emmanuel was born with missing limbs, and his body had not developed like other children's due to exposure to radioactive warheads commonly used in American weapons during the Iraq war. These warheads, designed to penetrate metal tanks, often leave behind radioactive materials that contaminate the ground where children once played and families lived. At the orphanage, Moira gently picked up Emmanuel and brought him back to Australia. Once home, many generous doctors and medical staff provided numerous surgeries and rehabilitation free of charge. This medical care allowed Emmanuel to access many of the things he could not have had in Iraq after the war. Moira went on to adopt Emmanuel and his brother Ahmed as her own children, raising them in a loving family environment. Moira knew to be a loving parent, a sacrifice was needed. Her sacrifices were not only financial, but were rooted in a deep willingness to go beyond what was expected and to enter places where love, and even the capacity to love, had been lost.

Sam and Ben

In 2007, Sam and his 20-year-old son Ben lived on a remote outback farm in Victoria. On one fateful Saturday afternoon, February 7, the Black Saturday fires struck. Ben returned home in his pickup truck. As he pulled up, towering flames, some 30 metres high, surrounded the property. The house where he and Sam lived for many years was already on fire. Something inside Ben told him, "Dad is inside." Without hesitation, he got out of his truck and entered the burning house. Despite the flames, Ben found his father unconscious in the middle of the house. He picked his dad up and carried him out to safety. As a result, Ben suffered burns to ten percent of his body, while Sam sustained burns to thirty percent.

The fire changed their relationship forever. Before the fire, Ben and Sam barely spoke. But afterward, everything shifted. They began to talk about things that truly mattered: relationships, sex, and their hopes for the future. There was something about facing death and loss that brought them closer together. The social researcher Brené Brown suggests that stepping into uncertainty is an act of sacrifice, in which one gives up emotional armour and embraces discomfort as a means of personal and communal transformation (Brown, pp. 34-36, 2012). For Sam and Ben, it was the Black Friday fires that changed them forever. In an instant, everything could be lost. Deep in their cores, they knew what truly mattered: human life. They knew that the love they had for each other was very important, but also this it could be easily lost.

Often, we do not know that we are deeply loved. There will be times in your life when you feel isolated, but these moments can also be opportunities for the deepest connection. The crisis that Sam and Ben experienced was an opportunity of how love can work. The sacrifices we make can help change our relationships. There is a difference between the love we feel as children and the love we experience as adults. Love is not just a feeling; it is a way of being. Many Indigenous cultures, such as those of Aboriginal Australians and North American First Nations, recognized this profound wisdom. They guide their children through various initiations and rites of passage in the wilderness, often involving the wider community and elders. Becoming an adult was not automatic. It did not just happen biologically because one reached a certain age. Today, we assume that turning 18 or 21 makes someone an adult. Becoming an adult requires us to develop both emotionally and spiritually, in connection with other people and adults, through the roles and relationships we play in family and community. We learn what it means to be an adult through the ups and downs, the good and the bad, of our lives. In these ancient cultures, adulthood meant being willing to sacrifice for those you love.

Abraham

The story of Abraham in the Old Testament may not strictly be a historical account, but can teach us about the importance of sacrifice. Around 2000 BCE, Abram, later called Abraham, was called by God to leave the prosperous city of Ur (Genesis 11:31; 12:1-4, NRSV). Ur was situated in eastern Iraq, where the Tigris and Euphrates Rivers Meet. Abram's family was quite wealthy, owning many sheep. Yet God asked Abram to leave everything he knew, and to follow God's calling. This would have seemed strange to his family, neighbours, and friends. Why would Abram leave everything he has spent a lifetime building? His wealth, his property, his family. This does not make sense.

After many years, Abraham and his wife conceived a child. This was a big deal in 4,000-year-old Middle Eastern culture. Children were a sign that the gods smiled on you. So, when God asked Abraham to sacrifice his son (Genesis 22:1–2, NRSV), the very fabric of Abraham's being would have shaken.

This was a profound test, as Abraham and his wife Sarah had longed for a child for many years. God was asking Abraham to give up the very thing he and Sarah had waited for with blood, sweat, and tears, a son. For most parents, such a request would be unthinkable. Strangely, Abraham followed God's request. Yet, at the last moment, an angel stopped Abraham.

Was this a test of Abraham's love for God? Or was it a revelation that God does not require such a blood sacrifice? Whatever the interpretation, this story reveals the profound connection between love and sacrifice. True love often calls us to surrender something deeply meaningful for the sake of something greater than the self.

Gianna Beretta

In 1961, Gianna Beretta, a paediatrician, was pregnant with her fourth child (Vatican, 2025). Gianna was then diagnosed with a large fibroma, a cancerous tumour in her uterus. Her doctors presented her with three options: first, to have a hysterectomy, which would remove the tumour but also end the life of her unborn child; second, to have an abortion, which would terminate the pregnancy; or third, to undergo a risky surgery to remove the tumour while trying to save the baby, knowing it could endanger her own life. Gianna chose the third option. The surgery was successful in removing the fibroma cancerous tumour, and on April 21, 1962, Gianna gave birth to a baby girl. Naming her Gianna Emanuela Molla. However, one week after giving birth, Gianna Beretta sadly died. Gianna's selfless decision saved her young child's life.

There is something inside of us that might resist the path that Gianna Beretta took. We want to continue living sometimes, despite the cost. Additionally, the Jewish spiritual book, the Talmud, calls us to consider a powerful statement about the value of human life and our call to love.

"Whoever destroys a single soul, it is as if he has destroyed the whole world; and whoever saves a single soul, it is as if he has saved the entire world" (from the Talmudic text Sanhedrin 4:5).

Life is sacred. Each person, whether young or old, reflects the deep mystery of God. There is a value which all of us hold, which some see while others do not. When we see this value, we are moved to love. This love often comes not through grand gestures but through small, simple steps in ordinary moments of our day. These moments frequently involve people right in front of us, those we may otherwise overlook. Yet, these seemingly ordinary actions can carry extraordinary power. When we respond to love in these small ways, we participate in something far greater than ourselves. For in showing love to one person, we help change the world.

Tuesdays with Morrie
The Film *"Tuesdays with Morrie"* (Jackson, 1999) depicts a successful sports journalist from the early 1980s. Living a busy lifestyle, constantly chasing one big news story after another. He has no time to pause and reflect. With deadlines looming, and the next big game to watch and write about. He barely even made time for his girlfriend, Janine. One day, Mitch heard that his old friend and beloved university professor, Morrie, was battling a devastating disease, Amyotrophic Lateral Sclerosis or ALS. Hesitant at first, Mitch decided to pay Morrie a random visit. Morrie welcomed him with open arms. Morrie spoke openly about life, relationships, vulnerability, and what truly mattered. Morrie reflected that many people chase material success while forgetting the deeper meaning of life: relationships. Morrie told Mitch, *"The most important thing in your life is to learn how to give out love, and to let it come back in"* (Jackson, 1999). He warned that

many fear vulnerability in relationships, but that true fulfillment comes from being vulnerable and selfless in their acts of love. Although Mitch listened, he did not initially accept Morrie's wisdom.

Mitch then decided to commit to visiting Morrie every Tuesday. Over time, Morrie taught Mitch profound life lessons. Slowly, Mitch's priorities begin to shift, from the demands of journalism to the meaningful Tuesday encounters with his former professor. A turning point occurred when Mitch opened up about his own struggles with commitment, particularly in his relationship with his girlfriend, Janine. In a powerful moment, Mitch invited his girlfriend to meet Morrie, and Morrie and Janine connected instantly. Through this experience, Mitch begins to understand that vulnerability in love is the pathways to deeper happiness. This newfound understanding transforms Mitch's relationship with Janine, bringing them closer together.

It can be difficult to live more authentically. To allow others to see us as we truly are, we must let go. There are barriers we create. Parker Palmer writes, *"Sacrifice is not about suffering, but choosing to live more authentically even when it is difficult"* (Palmer, p. 10, 2000). For many, the answer would be "no" or "I am not going to do that", it is much easier to go the other way, to follow the crowd and take the path of least resistance. The psychoanalyst James Hollis states, *"We must sacrifice societal expectations, false identities, and comfort to become our authentic selves"* (Hollis, 2003). What we think others expect of us often shapes who we are and what we do. But love calls us beyond these expectations and boundaries that keep us from truly knowing the other. Love reminds us that life is more than what we think or what others think. Life is about discovering our deeper selves and embracing this with love.

Fallen out of love

What happens when a married couple falls out of love? As children, or as a young couple, we may romanticize what love should look like. In older times, we might have imagined marrying the most beautiful person, our prince charming, seeking to have 2.5 children, a house, a car, and a job, representing the ultimate expression of true love. But, of course, we may eventually discover that dreams do not materialise. It happens that over time, some people fall out of love, at least in the ways they once knew it. The puppy love of early encounters or dating begins to feel distant and disconnected from what love truly requires. Esther Perel, a psychotherapist, suggests that we need to fall back into love (Perel, p. 37-42, 2006). In an age of constant distraction, giving our partner attention becomes crucial. Breaking routines with new experiences can rejuvenate our relationships. Perel explains that desire flourishes in space, and that openly discussing our deepest needs and desires can help reignite what has been lost.

Pope Benedict writes, *"The world offers you comfort, but you were not made for comfort. You were made for greatness"* (Benedict XVI, 2005). Love seeks to reveal who we truly are, the love of God living within us. This is at the heart of Christianity: the great mystery of Jesus living, dying, and God raising him from the dead three days later. This act of love reflects the very nature of God, one that transcends and moves beyond what is expected and normal to radically transform how we see the world. We are called to grow into a deeper, more mature love, one that moves beyond what is easy or comfortable and recognises the central place of sacrifice, both within ourselves and in how we love others.

The love you seek is not merely human love; it is divine love. *"God so loved the world that He gave His only Son"* (John 3:16). God the Father pours out His love upon the world through His Son. *"Greater love has no one than this: to lay down one's life for one's friends"* (John 15:13). Jesus hands his life back to his father through his death out of His deep love. But when Jesus returns, *"Jesus then breathed on them and said, 'Receive the Holy Spirit'"* (John 20:22). This love is ever flowing. The Father gives us his Son. The Son gives his life back to the Father. And as Saint Paul writes, *"Hope does not disappoint us, because God's love has been poured into our hearts through the Holy Spirit that has been given to us"* (Romans 5:5). The Holy Spirit becomes active in our lives through love, and this love is made possible when we truly open to God who is beyond us and beyond our recognition. This is called faith. God's love is poured out, and we, too, are called to pour out our love by letting go. The Trinity is a community of letting go through love, and we are invited to seek God's love: to become vessels of love. But we must remember, it is not merely our love we give, but God's love flowing through us as we participate in the loving action of God's love.

At the heart of every relationship lies an invitation to love beyond ourselves. True love is not found in what feels comfortable, but in our willingness to give, to let go, and to place the good of others before our own. It is through sacrifice that love deepens, relationships grow, and we begin to glimpse something that has remained hidden within our lives. We begin to rekindle the Christian flame when we seek to reflect God's love in our lives. Day by day, inch by inch, we come to know the love of God in the ordinary moments of our lives. Love transforms these moments so that they are no longer just ordinary but become sacred. Even in the darkness.

Journal

Spend 20 minutes journaling about the following.

Choose ONE of the following questions to journal about

1. *Dorothy Day's transformation began through the vulnerability of motherhood. Have there been moments in your life when vulnerability opened you up to a deeper sense of purpose or faith?*

2. *Sacrifice is a recurring theme in stories of love. What is one area of your life where you are being called to love more deeply?*

3. *Moira Kelly's compassion transformed the lives of Emmanuel and his brother, Ahmed. Who in your life has inspired you through their quiet acts of love? What impact did they have on you?*

4. *Brene Brown speaks of leaning into vulnerability. What fears or protective habits do you need to release in order to love?*

5. *Mitch Albom learned to slow down and listen through his Tuesdays with Morrie. Where in your own life might you need to slow down in order to reconnect with what truly matters?*

6. *Paul writes that faith, hope, and love remain, and the greatest is love. In what ways are you being called to express God's love in your everyday life, and what role do faith and hope play in shaping this direction?*

Journalling

Journalling

Journalling

Journalling

Prayer

Take a moment to pause.
　Close your eyes for two to three minutes.
　Become aware of your breathing.
　Breathe slowly.
　As you breathe in and as you breathe out.
　Afterwards, if it feels helpful, consider praying slowly this prayer in the days leading up to the next chapter.

Loving God,

You who call us to a love that gives, that sacrifices, that transforms, open our hearts to live with greater compassion and courage. May we, like Dorothy Day, who discovered You in the depths of love and vulnerability; like Gianna Beretta, who chose selflessness in the face of risk; like Moira Kelly, who responded with generosity to the suffering of others. Help us embrace the quiet, patient, daily acts of love; they help us navigate each challenging moment. Teach us to find You not in comfort, but in the greatness of service, surrender, and sacrifice. Amen.

Pause

Pause for one day or one week before going to the next chapter.

Allow the thoughts and ideas to sink in.

Reflect.

Ponder.

Journal.

Share with others.

Chapter Seven

The dark night

A poem by John of the Cross

"*On a dark night,*
  Kindled with love and yearnings,
Oh, happy chance,
I went forth unnoticed,
My house now being at rest.

In darkness and secure,
  By the secret ladder, disguised,
  Oh, happy chance,

My house now being at rest.

In that blessed night,
  In secret, when none saw me,
  Nor did I see,
  Without light or guide,
  Save that which burned in my heart." (John of the Cross, p35-37, 1959)

Desmond Dos

The true story of Desmond Doss, portrayed in the film Hacksaw Ridge (Gibson, 2016), powerfully illustrates the nature of the dark night and how the struggle can be transformed. Set during World War II, the film follows as a Seventh-day Adventist Christian is called to the war effort. What made Desmond Doss so usual was that he held very strong convictions about non-violence and pacifism. He refused to touch a gun or kill another person. During his army training, he was classified as a conscientious objector because of his refusal to bear arms. Desmond's commander urged him to leave the army, but Desmond stood firm in his beliefs to help with the war effort, but, not kill another person. He endured brutal beatings from fellow soldiers during training who saw his stance as a threat to national defence. Yet, Desmond remained committed to playing his part and caring for others, as a medic, driven by his deep Christian faith and the call to love other people.

During combat, on one dark night on the island of Okinawa, Japan, Desmond Doss's platoon was assigned the dangerous task of climbing a 130-metre cliff. Unknown to the American soldiers, waiting in sheer silence and the black of night on top were Japanese soldiers, ready to ambush the Americans. During the night, under heavy fire, hundreds of American soldiers were shot and killed. Many retreated back down the cliff in fear and chaos. But Desmond remained refusing to leave. In the darkness, Desmond found one American soldier still alive and wounded. Lifting the wounded soldier into his arms Desmond carried him to the edge of the cliff and carefully lowered him down very slowly to safety. Then Desmond returned into the dark of night. He went out again to find another soldier, and carried him to, to the edge of the cliff. Over, and over again, Desmond returned to the battlefield, rescuing one wounded soldier at a time. After each rescue, he prayed, "Lord, let me get one more." That night, Desmond saved 75 soldiers, one by one. Remaining undetected by the Japanese soldiers. He later explained, "Because I love you, I will care for you, even if it means risking my life." Despite the beatings he endured during training, the opposition of his commander, and the threat of death, Desmond was willing to give his life to rescue other injured soldiers.

Catherine of Siena, in the 16th century, spoke extensively about the Christian struggle (Kerr, 2009). Catherine believed that enduring struggle was necessary for achieving spiritual maturity. For Desmond Dos this road meant committing to an army which did not want to accept his pacifist ways and risking the threat of gun fire to save another soldier's life. For Catherine, the dark night and struggles were not obstacles but stepping-stones toward a deeper relationship with God. The dark night helped to purify her soul. She emphasized the importance of enduring trials with love rather than bitterness or despair, viewing love as the ultimate motivator for accepting life's challenges.

When we are faced with struggles today, we sometimes run away. Not wanting to face the hardship and reality we prefer the easier road than the more difficult road. We can sometimes pop pills to avoid the pain or can turn to substances in our attempt to numb our senses. We can give in to peer pressure just to feel connected. In our relationships sometimes a lover may allow themselves to be used as an object of lust or desire, clinging to the need to be loved. But John of the Cross's poem offers a radically different way through. He calls the darkness good. He refers to life's challenges as a "happy chance," as if there is richness and hidden treasure is the very things we typically try to avoid. He sees the yearnings and longings of the heart not as burdens, but as sacred opportunities. For Desmond Dos it was precisely heading back into the physical dark night which enabled him to save 75 lives.

Like the dark night, deserts of our lives are the places we often avoid, the barren spaces of uncertainty, discomfort, and hardship. When the Israelites escaped the tyranny of slavery in Egypt around 1200 BCE, they found themselves in the wilderness, only to cry out to Moses, *"Let us appoint a leader and return to Egypt"* (Numbers 14:4). Despite their suffering, Egypt was familiar. The desert, though a path to freedom, felt overwhelming, unknown and a place of death. Similarly, in our own lives, we may long to retreat to what is familiar, even if it enslaves us in a spiritual sense, rather than face the discomfort of change.

Jesus' journey into the desert marks a pivotal moment at the start of his ministry and mission. Led by the Spirit, he enters a place of solitude and testing, where the devil attempts to distort reality, presenting falsehoods as truths to divert him from his divine mission (Matthew 4:1–11). In our own lives, we encounter similar "deserts", periods of hardship and uncertainty where our usual strategies falter. These moments challenge us to confront discomfort and grow beyond our limitations. But there can be goodness even in the desert. The desert can cause us to think more deeply. The desert strips away illusions, compelling us to rely not on our plans or societal comforts, but on a deeper trust in God's guidance. Though our culture often urges us to seek quick fixes or return to familiar comforts, the desert experience invites transformation, teaching us to depend on every word that comes from the mouth of God (Matthew 4:4).

Are we willing to go into the desert in our lives?

A poem - Deserts way

"When I was born,
The red dust already knew my name.
The wind carved stories in the sand,
Long before the white man's ways.
The desert is not empty,
Though untrained eyes may say so.
It whispers deep meaning in the stillness of rolling lands.
We absorb it, and it becomes part of us.

The sun seems harsh, and water lost,
But every sign is a guide:
The spinifex, the willy-wagtail,
The trails left by a snake,
They hide.

We follow tracks unseen by most,
Of wallaby,
Of goanna,
Of little feet that stammer.

At night, the desert comes alive:
Great movement.
The cool dew, a hidden source of water.
My mother showed me how to gather.

My father showed me how to hunt,
Teaching the hidden truths of how to live in the desert.

Not in the hot sun,
But in the sacred night,
Where what seems absent comes alive.

The sun will burn,
But the night is a hidden treasure
Waiting for us to realise
It is really pleasure". (The author)

To survive in the desert, both the physical challenges we face, but also the spiritual crisis where life falls apart, can we find a way through? For Christians, faith seems to provide a doorway. Anselm of Canterbury, in the 11th century, expressed this with the phrase "fides quaerens intellectum or "faith seeking understanding", emphasizing that belief precedes comprehension (Anselm of Canterbury, as cited in the Stanford Encyclopedia of Philosophy). Notice that Anslem puts faith first. Before knowledge. Today, often, look in school, we may approach issues faith with knowledge first. What we think comes first, rather than what we trust in what we do not see.

Darkness, often perceived as negative, holds profound significance. In the vast expanse of the universe, darkness dominates, approximately ninety five percent consists of dark matter and dark energy, with visible matter making up only about five percent (European Space Agency). This unseen majority shapes the cosmos, reminding us that the most influential forces are often invisible. In space this is the darkness.

Similarly, our thought process or our egos resist relinquishing control, clinging to certainty. Yet, in the desert, both literal and metaphorical, our egos are stripped away, revealing our true selves.

Our minds and emotions often deceive us as we attempt to navigate life's challenges. The psychologist Carl Jung termed this the "shadow", the unconscious aspects of our personality that we reject or deny (Jung, 1951/1979, p285). These elements, which we prefer to keep hidden, may not always be sinful but can include the narratives we tell ourselves to justify psychological patterns or complexes that hinder our acceptance of reality. Jung emphasized that acknowledging and integrating the shadow is crucial for achieving wholeness (Jung, 1951/1979, p. 285; Jung, 1958/1973, pp. 131-132). Do we venture to open our hearts into the unknown to help us understand our shadow self?

In the spiritual life this question is more than the shadow self as seen in psychology. John of the Cross described these moments as a "Dark Night of the Soul" or a period of spiritual desolation where both the senses and the spirit feel abandoned by God (1990). This experience is not merely about external hardships but involves a profound internal purification, leading the soul toward a deeper union with the Divine (Prodigal Catholic, 2019). The way through is not what we think or what our minds have determined. Rather the way through is the way we prefer not to go. We can be purified not by what we do but by the journey of our life and God's hidden hand who helps us through.

In these dark nights, our usual ways of understanding and coping can fail us. Our plans and cultural solutions offer little solace. Yet, it is in these moments of darkness that change, and transformation occurs. By confronting and embracing our shadows, we open ourselves to growth and a more authentic connection with God (Prodigal Catholic, 2019). This is not just about accepting sin or the injustices we face. Rather it is confronting the reality in our lives head on. In the dark nights which we face in our lives, can we find our own way through by what we do not see or hear?

In the desert, God can form us. God can strip away our illusions and invites us into deeper trust. The wilderness is not a punishment, but a passage. A sacred space where initiation into life often begins.

In Islam, the concept of the desert is closely tied to the idea of struggle, or jihad. While jihad is often misunderstood as the emphasis on outward struggles like external conflict or violence, rather, in Islam, the deeper meaning of jihad is our internal struggles. The greater jihad is the spiritual battle within us. The hidden part of who we are. This greater struggle is against sin, temptation, and the ego's desire for control.

Within Islam, the Sufi tradition seeks to overcome or pass through these inner struggles. Sufis speak of nafs such as the ego which is seen as a series of obstacles that include selfish desires and attachments that may hinder following God's way. The renowned Sufi scholar Al-Ghazali explores this process in The Revival of the Religious Sciences, describing how, through a series of stages, a person can move from a state of desire to one of harmony with the divine will (Al-Ghazali, 1993). As we reflect on our lives, we can sometimes see stages of psychological and spiritual growth. Stages where we have woken up. Where the desert of our lives is not simply struggle but the pages in our own story where we have learnt something deeply spiritual despite the obstacles we have experienced.

What are the obstacles we experience? They can be different and many.

When Mother Teresa first came to Australia, she felt pity for Australians, seeing them as very poor, not in material terms, but spiritually. She observed that our material wealth had become an obstacle to entering the

Kingdom of God. Like the rich man that Jesus tells in Luke's Gospel who approaches Jesus asking, *"What must I do to inherit eternal life?"* (Luke 18:18-30, NRSV). In our modern culture we often equate happiness with money and pleasure. Jesus responds by listing several commandments, to which the rich man quickly replies, *"I have kept all of these".* (18:21). But the one thing the rich man had not done, Jesus intentionally left off the list for him to do. Hoping that the rich man might see and learn for himself. Good teachers will not simply give you the answer, but create a pathway for personal learning. The rich man does not. Jesus responds *"Go, sell all that you own and give the money to the poor, and you will have treasure in heaven. Then come, follow me"* (18:22). Yet the rich man walks away. We are like the rich man. We think our wealth is part of God's divine plan, or we justify why we need to hold onto our wealth. We do not see that wealth can be a block to God. We would rather walk away than give up our wealth. To truly trust in God requires a us to surrender and let go of everything.

In the dark of night, Jesus sits down with a prominent Jewish rabbi, Nicodemus in John Chapter 3. Scholars may think Nicodemus did not want to be publicly seen with Jesus, so he came by night. Nicodemus, and says, *"Very truly I tell you, no one can enter the Kingdom of God without being born from above".* Nicodemus is confused: "How can anyone be born after growing old? Can one enter a second time into the mother's womb?" Jesus replies, *"No one can enter the Kingdom of God without being born of water and Spirit. What is born of the flesh is flesh, and what is born of the Spirit is spirit"* (John 3:5–6). The darkness is no longer just physical or a matter of time of day for Nicodemus, but has become something spiritual he cannot comprehend or see through. Nicodemus seems to be confused by what Jesus is proposing.

The main message is that surrendering to God begins with inner transformation and deep submission to God's will. This surrender brings rest to the soul, as we enter God's presence. By letting go of sins, hurts, worries, fears, and attachments, we find that only God's presence remains. No longer struggling to hold ourselves together, we are gently carried by grace. Like a single drop of water merging into the vast ocean, we remain ourselves, yet are fully enveloped in a love too deep to measure, immersed in an endless ocean of God's mercy and life.

In the darkness of our own night, we too must sit with Jesus to reflect on what is truly keeping us from entering the Kingdom of God. At times, we may slip back into our old ways. But God's mercy is infinitely willing to forgive. The purpose of the darkness is not punishment, but revelation. God speaks even through the dark. We can interpret darkness negatively, as sin. But darkness is so much more than sin. On our journey through life, we may lose our way or fail to see the way forward. When we look back on life, we may see different types of darkness as stepping stones, helping us find a deeper truth that was hidden or missing. Navigating in the darkness, not with answers, but with further questions, which can help us to integrate the darkness in our own lives.

As described in the book of Genesis, around 4000 years ago, Jacob also had an encounter at night. Overwhelmed with anxiety and fear as he prepares to confront his brother Esau, as he wants to talk about their father's inheritance. When someone has either died or is reaching old age, family wealth can tear a family apart. Jacob sends his family across the river and remains alone to face this struggle. In the pitch black of night, with no moon, a mysterious man finds Jacob and begins to wrestle with him. The scripture reads *"So, Jacob was left alone, and a man wrestled with him until daybreak"* (Genesis 32:24). Jacob wrestles with this strange figure. At some point, Jacob's hip is dislocated, and he receives a wound. In the darkness, Jacob's struggle becomes more than a physical fight; it becomes a sacred and inner wrestling of the soul, where fear, surrender, and faith collide.

It is often in our deepest night, when we dare to wrestle with God rather than run from Him, that we are wounded, changed, and finally blessed like Jacob.

Even Jesus wrestles with God. While on the cross, He cries out, *"My God, my God, why have you abandoned me?"* (Matthew 27:46, Mark 15:34, NRSV). Jesus is only taken down from the cross after He dies. The sky turns dark only after His death. It is only in the darkness that the suffering ceases. We may experience stages in our darkness, such as avoidance, bargaining with God, or depression. Depression is not just a clinical or psychological depression. Depression describes a spiritual state where our soul is weighed down, numb, or cut off from the light. Like a winter when prayer may feel dry, God feels silent, and hope seems absent. This is not simply sadness but a deeper spiritual weariness.

It is very difficult to capture the depth of darkness, as there are different levels to the darkness. In the spiritual darkness we face, there may be questions or a desire to search for something more. Yet darkness has a way of shutting off our senses and perceptions. To see in the darkness can feel impossible.

The more extreme the darkness we encounter, the more likely we are to push it down or avoid the reality of what it truly is. We suppress these struggles, and in doing so, we may become depressed or deeply emotional. Sometimes, people prefer to remain in the darkness, whether it be addictions or distorted ways of interpreting life, rather than trust in an unknown path forward.

Darkness can also resemble an abyss. It is not always about what we do, but rather what has been done to us. When loved ones are suddenly taken from us in death, or when people face a sickness that cannot be healed, they are surrounded by a darkness that goes beyond words. In the film *"What Dreams May Come"* (Ward, 1998), Annie (Annabella Sciorra) loses her two children and later her husband, Chris Nielsen (Robin Williams), in separate car accidents. Annie, distraught by the loss of her entire family, tragically takes her own life. Instead of arriving in heaven, she enters what can be described as an abyss. Paradoxically, even beyond death, Chris longs to reunite with his soul mate in the afterlife. As Chris searches for Annie in the afterlife, he is told that Annie is not in hell but in a place beyond explanation, an abyss where she is lost. The guides, or some would call angels, who assist Chris explain that no words can truly describe where Annie is. Despite knowing that Annie will not recognize him in this abyss, Chris chooses to go and find Annie.

In the book *"Gift of the Red Bird"*, Paula D'Arcy (1996) describes losing her daughter and husband in a car accident. She details the true story of the immense loss and grief she experienced after the tragedy. Paula's life was also marked by great devastation. Later, during a solitary camping retreat in the wilderness of Colorado, Paula faced a massive storm at night with fierce wind, lightning, and rain, and thought she was going to die. It was precisely at this moment in the abyss of night that Paula surrendered her entire life and existence to a higher power. Then, everything changed. The dark night passed.

The Alcoholics Anonymous program teaches that often when people have truly hit rock bottom that they begin to search for a higher power. This higher power becomes a source of strength and healing, guiding them through the recovery process. However, in our own spiritual journey, we may not have reached this point. Until we have reached rock bottom, until we are truly ready, or when we are "poor in spirit" that we could try and seek something greater beyond us. Sometimes, we may need to make a cocoon for ourselves and spend more time in the darkness. Like in the dead of winter, we may long for spring or summer to arrive early, but the reality is that we may still be in the middle of our winter. The winter seasons of our life may not yet have past, and we may need to wait patiently for the processes of life to take its course.

There is something greater than the human self in the dark night, something we cannot control. It may cause us to suffer, to fall apart, to enter an abyss, and even to die.

Jesus teaches: *"Very truly I tell you, unless a grain of wheat falls into the earth and dies, it remains just a single grain. But if it dies, it produces much fruit"* (John 12:24, NRSV). This is not simply another metaphor. There is something profoundly human about the dark night, something that cannot be explained by mere words but only understood through experience.

The way forward is not to offer an answer, but to ask a question: "Are we open to experiencing the dark night?" and "do we surrender?"

Journal

Spend some time, maybe 20 minutes, journaling about the following

Choose ONE of the following questions to journal about

1. What is one "darkness" or "desert" in your life right now?

2. Have you experienced a "dark night" of the soul?

3. What are you holding onto that keeps you from surrendering more fully to a higher power?

4. What struggles have wounded you and how might those wounds be openings to grace, like Jacob's limp or Jesus' cross?

5. Are you aware of avoidance, anger, bargaining, depression, or acceptance in your life? Which of Kübler-Ross's five stages resonates most with your current situation, and why?

6. What types of darkness do people face? Why do people often remain in their darkness?

7. What do these questions mean to you: "Are we open to experiencing the dark night?" and "do we surrender?"

Journalling

Journalling

Journalling

Journalling

Prayer

Take a moment to pause.
  Close your eyes for two to three minutes.
  Become aware of your breathing.
  Breathe slowly.
  As you breathe in and as you breathe out.
  Afterwards, if it feels helpful, consider praying slowly this prayer in the days leading up to the next chapter.

Loving God,
in the darkness and deserts of our lives, when the path is uncertain and the night feels long, help us to trust that You are near. Teach us to see our struggles not as signs of failure but as invitations to deeper faith. Like Jacob, may we wrestle honestly with You; like Desmond, may we serve with courage and love; and like Catherine of Siena, may we endure trials with a heart aflame for You. In our darkest moments, may we remember that even the shadow is filled with Your light, even though it may seem dark. Strip away all that is false within us, and lead us into the quiet transformation that comes only through surrender. Let our wounds become wells of gentleness and compassion. May our darkness become the sacred place where we meet You.
Amen.

Pause

Pause for one day or one week before going to the next chapter.

    Allow the thoughts and ideas to sink in.

    Reflect.

    Ponder.

    Journal.

    Share with others.

Chapter Eight

Darkness cannot drive out darkness - Martin Luther Jr

A Poem - The darkest night

"In valleys where the shadows stay,
　　Where hatred and violence plant their roots each dark day,
A candle flickers, small and bright,
Yet still it shatters deepest night.

The voices rage, the tempers flare,
Deep down, emotions I will not bear.
Sin is hidden,

Sin, I will not declare.

Running and running and running,
Fear paints my sky the darkest of night.
But love, not wrath, brings healing there.
No sword of vengeance ever mends
What mercy soothes, what kindness bends.
Though hate may raise its harshest cry,
Stronger still will love testify?

The dawn is coming,
In faith.
There is light at the end of the tunnel.
Let light break through, transforming despair.
And scatter peace into the air.
Love beyond all knowing,
Love awakens us.
To see within the darkness.
Sin is there,
But now, as Paul once said:
"Love abides more." I declare". (The author)

The topic of sin seems to be out of fashion. Shadow might sound like a cooler word for sin, but even that has lost its edge. It's like ordering chips from a burger shop. Without the chicken salt, they lose their zing. We can avoid talking about uncomfortable topics, especially those that belong behind closed doors, or the addictions that we just can't seem to shake. Culturally, it's easy to think, "I have every right to be greedy, envious, lustful, lazy, or prideful, just as long as I don't bother anyone else. And if anyone dares confront us? How dare you speak to me about that? It's none of your business."

The Church's voice on sin is often completely dismissed, especially because of the historical sexual abuse by some clergy or religious, which may have caused deep and lasting harm. Sin has become an ancient word or a word that is part of a conversation taboo. Maybe we're tempted to stop using it altogether because the concept of sin feels too burdensome, too complicated, too confronting.

Sin may not be the same as darkness. Christians see sin as doing the opposite of the goodness that people may bring to God or others. The Ten Commandments (Exodus 20, NRSV) provide a foundation for how people are called to relate to one another. Ethics like *"Thou shalt not steal"* (Exodus 20:15, NRSV), *"thou shalt not commit adultery"* (Exodus 20:14), or *"thou shalt not envy"* (Exodus 20:17, NRSV) cause the Christian to ponder, *"how am I treating other people"*? The point is not just the principle of what is right from wrong, but rather, have we missed something? Sin has a habit of hiding like the serpent who strangely makes his way in the garden of Eden (Genesis 3:1, NRSV). Sin tries to stay hidden. This hidden dimension of sin, or the effect of sin itself, may create a darkness.

As we explored the themes of the abyss in the last Chapter, we may also find that darkness is beyond our control. Like natural evils, when people get terminally sick or a tragic accident occurs, a darkness might have entered our lives. This darkness could have the same effect. We are surrounded by darkness, but we can get out of it.

Martin Luther King Jr. once wrote, *"Darkness cannot drive out darkness; only light can do that. Hate cannot drive out hate; only love can do that"* (King, p. 53, 1963). When we point fingers to accuse others, are we missing something? It is easier to accuse others. To speak behind people's backs about what the problem is. Maybe the "zing" in the chips is not others, but rather, what we are missing or choosing to avoid in our own lives. Jesus says, *"Why do you see the speck in your neighbour's eye, but do not notice the log in your own eye? Or how can you say to your neighbour, 'Let me take the speck out of your eye,' while the log is in your own eye?"* (Matthew 7:3, NRSV). This is easier said than done. How do we get that zing back? Even if we ignore the Church, is sin still sin? Is evil still evil? The answer depends on who you ask and what you ask. For the scientist, it is through science that we overcome scientific problems. For the teacher and student, it is through learning that we overcome ignorance. For the doctor and patient, it is through medicine that healing comes. For the musician, it is through music that harmony is restored. But for the Christian, it is through the person of Jesus Christ. Jesus taught, *"I am the way, the truth, and the life"* (John 14:6, NRSV).

The Abdallah story

On one tragic afternoon, Saturday, February 1st, 2020, at around 4 p.m., five children were walking along a quiet suburban street in Oatlands, on the outskirts of Sydney. They were on their way to buy ice cream. Tragically, a car mounted the curb and struck the group, killing Antony (aged 13), Angelina (aged 12), Sienna (aged 12), and their cousin Veronique (aged 11). The driver was under the influence of both drugs and alcohol. This heartbreaking event shocked the nation, as such innocent and beautiful lives were taken in an instant. No words can express the deep sadness this event evoked, not only for the family but also for those who hear this story. No words can convey this sadness. Only tears.

We struggle to explain suffering.

From a scientific or biological perspective, we can observe what happens when people consume excessive amounts of alcohol or take drugs. We can ask further questions, such as why, from a psychological perspective, people become addicted to substances. Perhaps they have experienced significant trauma or abuse in childhood. Yet science can only take us so far. The deeper question is, why do such events happen? We struggle to make meaning from these terrible events. We may even question the existence of God. Where is God in the face of such suffering?

If God is so powerful, why does He not stop the deaths of millions? Elie Wiesel, a Holocaust survivor, wrestled with the silence of God during the Holocaust. He witnessed firsthand the hanging of a child in a concentration camp and recalled someone shouting, *"Where is God now?"* Wiesel responded, *"Here he is. He is hanging on the gallows"* (Wiesel, p. 65, 2006). Another survivor, Viktor Frankl, offered a different insight. He suggested that *"Where is God?"* is not the right question. Rather, we should ask, "Where is human beings when faced with great suffering?" This opens other important reflections, such as the role of free will in the face of tragedy. Frankl argues that every person is free to choose how to respond, even in the most horrific circumstances (Frankl, p. 65, 2006). This does not make us feel better when faced with great tragedy.

Pain and Suffering

The question of pain and suffering cannot be fully explained in this life. We do not want pain to lead to more pain, but often it does. Can we learn to hold our suffering rather than escape it? Perhaps it has something to teach us? This does not erase the reality of pain. Rather, it invites us to consider that there may be something more, a deeper meaning, even within the suffering itself.

God is a healer. God desires to heal not only the victim, but also the one causing the pain. Deep down there is something inside of us that calls out to life beyond death and hope beyond suffering. If we believe in life beyond death, we must recognize that how we live now matters, not only in this world but in the world to come.

On February 1st, 2020, in response to the tragic loss of their children at Oatlands, Sydney, the Abdallah parents demonstrated profound mercy. Leila Abdallah, the mother, publicly declared, "I forgive the driver. I can't hate him. I think in my heart to forgive him, but I want the court to be fair." We ask ourselves, "How is this possible? How can a parent respond with such forgiveness in the face of unimaginable tragedy?" Each of us might hold sadness and anger towards this event. How does each person respond with forgiveness? Like John Wayne in a Western movie, we try to face life with a steely gaze, guns drawn, and a tough voice. For Danny and Leila Abdallah they responded with love. For many, this does not make sense.

Why is it that those who follow God often suffer? Why is suffering part of the human condition? When we are born at the beginning of our lives, there is great suffering. As the mother undergoes hours and hours of labour. When we die, people often die through great suffering. Why do we think that suffering, which exists at the beginning and end of life, would not be part of the middle of our lives?

God does not avoid human pain but actively enters into it. God's own Son was scourged and executed by one of the most brutal methods of execution in human history. The Roman Empire at that time oppressed any sense of resistance or disorder. They would not hesitate to execute anyone who would question their version of Roman peace or PAX Roma. Like Jesus, other Christians, Peter and Paul, were executed by the Romans. The three great figures who laid the foundation of Christianity suffered greatly. There is something deep within us that pleads for these acts not to be true. The injustice they faced, and that so many others have faced, seems unbearable. Surely, we think, this cannot be part of God's design.

The Psalmist wrote, *"Surely the darkness shall cover me, and the light around me become night, even the darkness is not dark to you, for darkness is as light as the day"* (Psalm 139:12, NRSV). No place is hidden from God. Could we be the ones who do the hiding? It is difficult to define darkness. Even after all, we cannot see darkness. It is dark. How can we see in the dark?

Trying to make sense of light and dark

In his book *"The God Delusion"*, Richard Dawkins (2005) most likely does not view evil as an objective reality, but rather evil defined as a subjective human concept. However, we don't have to look far to see the devastating effects of evil both subjectively and objectively. We see the destruction cancer brings, the chaos caused by war, and the trauma inflicted by domestic violence. We can examine brain scans that reveal how pornography addiction alters the mind. We can measure the loss of access to clean water due to climate change. These are not just subjective experiences, but they can be applied across different groups of people. Their effects can be measured. Through logic and reason, we can draw our objective truths from subjective observations. These principles of the subjective to the objective can also be applied to God. To the study of God. Theology. But it is hard to clearly see things in theology as we do in science.

Through the lens of science, we can clearly differentiate between natural events, such as disasters, and moral evil, which results from poor human choices. Moral evil is directly caused by human actions or inactions. Humans have the capacity to choose between good and bad, and to commit sin such as murder. Conversely, natural evil is beyond human choice, such as earthquakes, tsunamis, diseases, and droughts. In ancient cultures, however, these two types of evil were often conflated. People believed that natural disasters were a direct result of human actions or human sin.

Good and evil are not always opposite forces locked in battle; they are deeply interconnected. Can goodness emerge from evil? Can evil arise from what was once good? The answer, perhaps uncomfortably, is yes. When people suffer, like the Abdallah family who lost their children, there is something that cries out to us to reach out to them and embrace them with our own arms. The love that reigns in our hearts we want to extend to them. Saying the words "I am sorry". This love moves beyond mere words. Embracing the experience with love, gentleness, and mercy enables us to move through great tragedy. We might only see what is on the surface. Love can enable us to be more patient. In great stillness and a time of waiting, there may eventually appear a way through.

Overcoming darkness and evil

Paradoxically, it may be that within the darkness, our eyes adjust, and the light becomes all the more visible. When the Jewish people were taken into exile in 587BCE, away from their promised land, some of the greatest Biblical prophets, God's messengers, appeared to light the way. The prophet Ezekiel writes, *"I will give you a new heart and put a new spirit in you; I will remove your heart of stone and give you a heart of flesh"* (36:26, NRSV). Similarly, the prophet Jeremiah writes, *"for I know the plans I have for you, declares the Lord, plans for your welfare, and not for evil, to give you a future and a hope"* (29:11, NRSV). Both passages respond to the darkness of the Jewish people when in prison and captivity. God reminds us of goodness despite the darkness through these Biblical prophets. Similarly, today, through the Abdallah family, we see God speak through the love they bring in their mercy. The goodness that appears reflects the goodness of Jesus, who on the cross declares, *"Father, forgive them. They know not what they do"* (Luke 23:34, NRSV).

The Psalmist writes, *"even the darkness is not dark to you, and the night is as bright as the day"* (Psalm 139:12, NRSV). This does not mean we twist reality or glorify evil, as if self-flagellation or sin were good. No. But when we are facing our greatest despair, in the midst of our dark nights, something deep within us can awaken to the truth that there is more. When facing darkness, we must realise that what we see is not the whole picture. This is not the whole picture! As Jesus, God's son, cries out dying on the cross, *"My God, my God, why have you abandoned me?"* (Matthew 27:46; Mark 15:34; NRSV) It is not God who abandons us. Perhaps it is we who have abandoned God.

Christianity teaches that God became human so that we might truly know Him. In a deeply personal and intimate way, God desires to be part of our lives, even the parts we try to hide. God entered into our humanity not as an abstract idea, but as a real person. The person of Jesus Christ. Later in the Gospel, when Jesus stands in the temple towards the beginning of his ministry, he reads from the scroll of the prophet Isaiah, *"The Spirit of the Lord is upon me, for He has anointed me to proclaim good news to the poor"* (Luke 4:18, NRSV), He is speaking directly to us. We are the poor. We are the blind. We are the oppressed. We are in darkness. And Jesus comes to bring us healing, hope, and true freedom. Saying to us *"I am with you"* (Matthew 28:20, NRSV).

Journal

Spend 20 minutes journaling about the following.

Choose ONE of the following questions to journal about

1. *Where do you see the effects of evil in the world, both natural and moral, and how have you personally responded to them?*

2. *Have you ever witnessed someone respond to tragedy with profound forgiveness, like Leila and Danny Abdallah? Why or why not?*

3. *When in your life have you seen goodness emerge from evil?*

4. *In moments of darkness, despair, or doubt, how do you experience God's presence, if at all?*

5. *Can darkness draw people closer to each other or God? Why?*

6. *Jesus reads in the temple, "The Spirit of the Lord is upon me, for He has anointed me to proclaim good news to the poor" (Luke 4:18, NRSV). What does that mean for your own life?*

7. *Matthew writes "I am with you" (28:20, NRSV). Where is He?*

Journalling

Journalling

Journalling

Journalling

Prayer

Take a moment to pause.
   Close your eyes for two to three minutes.
   Become aware of your breathing.
   Breathe slowly.
   As you breathe in and as you breathe out.
   Afterwards, if it feels helpful, consider praying slowly this prayer in the days leading up to the next chapter.

Loving and merciful God,
In a world where evil is often silenced and suffering misunderstood, open our hearts to Your truth. Help us to see not only the darkness around us, but also our misunderstandings. Teach us to walk with courage through the darkness, trusting that even there, You are near. Like the prophets of old, stir in us a longing for justice, a spirit to find deeper truth, and a willingness to forgive like your son Jesus. Remind us, Lord, that healing begins not with perfection, but with honesty and connection, with You and with one another. May we find in Your light the strength to face what is dark, and with patience, guide us through. Amen.

Pause

Pause for one day or one week before going to the next chapter.
    Allow the thoughts and ideas to sink in.
    Reflect.
    Ponder.
    Journal.
    Share with others.

Chapter Nine

The road to authenticity

A Reflection - A more authentic apple

"When I was a teenager, in Year Eleven,
I wandered the school halls of what I was becoming.
One lunch, I'd slip into the upstairs computer room,
A place where screens were only for teenage boys to view.

Five gathered, loud with grins and desire made clear,
Their laughter was sharp, their minds like they had speared.
On glowing glass, they gazed at a woman made bare,
Images falsely claimed I could possess.

I did not truthfully stand, I did not speak,
Instead, I followed, lost and weak.
A silence settled in my soul,
A crack that widened,
consumed my lips.

For years, that moment echoed in my mind,
My heart bowed low beneath true value.
I chased the world, its glittered dream.
Fast cars, fame, my selfish scheme.

As a boy,
I tried possessing,
But found an immature wildness.
Pretending to be more,
A decaying apple core.
Though I thought
A delicious taste.

I did not see the deeper cry,
The wounds I buried that made me shy,
The self-esteem would never fly,
The pain that pressed me to wear the Serpent's mask
The apple I chose in the past.

But as time went on,
I discovered a hint of grace,
Where wiser men and women gathered,

It would set my path straight.
A different place.
On a Spiritual farm on the far rolling hills.
A type of church.
I was invited to,
read the book "Manhood",
and shared and prayed.
Discovering a deeper truth
The real journey
Humble
Gentle
Willingness
Not seek
that dry apple core
but to protect it.

It was through the struggle.
That I turned the page.
Of knowing
Wisdom which
acknowledged
and revealed the real
of what took place.

Not for power, pride, or a sleazy show,
Not in shadow or some dark place.
The value of who I was
infinitely more than holding an apple core.
The eyes are called to heaven,

But, not just the height of the ceiling in those school halls.
But, to look to the stars.
Through the darkness.
Well beyond what I saw.
A truer calling.
To admire the beauty,
of the apple
and respecting and cherishing.

To let my soul, torn, yes, it is,
be healed, mended,
I sowed fig leaves for my thoughts and feelings.
By each moment of grace.
My true self slowly emerged.
By grace,
in struggle,
To journey on, to navigate through the night.
Becoming something, beyond delight.

Reminded that I am a child of God, with voice and name,
Called to reflect God's infinite grace,
and not some rotten apple illusion,
In the Garden of Eden,
But
In humility
In newfound willingness
Accepting my struggle
Reaching for the stars
With each step,

a more authentic life.
Revealing that I, too, am an apple.
In God's Garden,
Where all apples need
to be protected,
and cared for
and infinitely 'Blessed' ". (The author)

Who are you called to be? Our world today tends to prioritise the individual. What the individual wants, the individual gets. What the ego wants, the ego gets. To reinforce this false truth, our culture places into our hands the tools we use to become our presumed authentic self, or what we think our authentic self is. This façade does not last very long, because soon we will discover another product or image which we will desire: an endless cycle of becoming something else.

For younger people, it is very hard to find an authentic pathway in life against the obstacles of what we or others want us to become. Our culture can dictate how we should dress, how we should speak and what we should do. The image of ourselves is by our own design or the design a culture has set for us. In a world where every flaw can be photoshopped away, what happens to the beauty and truth of what we cannot see? What the world doesn't tell us is that perfection isn't a destination; it is a deception to get us to buy their product or follow their expectation. What the world doesn't tell us is that it uses desire as its marketing strategy. Yet no matter how much we buy, achieve, or refine, a deep void within us remains unfilled. We've become prisoners in an impossible game of looking good and appearing perfect, trapped in a cycle of self-doubt and false images. What if the real problem isn't that we are flawed, but that we believe we should not be flawed?

The Perks of Being a Wallflower

In the film The Perks of Being a Wallflower (Chbosky, 2012), we follow Charlie, a 15-year-old high school student struggling to fit in. Charlie is a socially anxious introvert. He wrestles with loneliness, trauma, and depression. At the beginning of the film, it is thought that he does not fit in anywhere. He seems not to have any friends. In his English class, his teacher, Mr Anderson, notices that Charlie is very smart but hides away, not wanting to engage in learning. His English teacher, Mr Anderson, introduces him to literature as an emotional outlet, and Charlie eagerly takes to it. Soon, Charlie's life begins to change when he befriends Patrick, an openly gay senior, and Sam, Patrick's sister, accepts Charlie for who he is, warts and all. Charlie feels comfortable with Patrick and Sam, who help him to break out of his introverted shell. As Charlie grows closer to them, his past resurfaces, revealing deeply repressed memories, a sense of low self-worth, and the recent suicide of his best friend. Sam is initially shaken by the news that Charlie's friend recently committed suicide and wants to support Charlie even more. Despite these positive changes, Charlie's trauma lingers just below the surface. When Sam leaves school for college, unresolved memories of his aunt Helen's abusive life begin to fall apart even more, which triggers a mental breakdown. Charlie is hospitalised, and for the first time, he begins to openly confront his pain. Through this downward journey, Charlie learns that while his past will always be part of him, it does not make him unworthy of love or happiness.

Each of us may have been like Charlie at some point in our lives, where we feel like we do not fit in, where people may take advantage of us, or we may have been abused. Maybe we have found a group of friends to support us through this. But then again, maybe not. We can suppress our authentic selves to fit in with the crowd and just survive. School especially, can be a place where social pressures and peer pressure can overwhelm us. It is hard to be our authentic selves in environments which may not have our best intentions in mind, environments where bullying, judgment and social acceptance take centre stage. How do we navigate these moments? When do we not have sufficient internal resources, like self-esteem and self-worth, to navigate the avenues of our lives?

Good Will Hunting

In the film Good Will Hunting (Van Sant, 1997), Robin Williams (as the counsellor Sean) and Matt Damon (as a young adult Will) explore the struggle to be their authentic selves. As a child, Will has endured a lifetime of pain, growing up in several violent and traumatic houses marked by both physical and emotional abuse. Will was passed from one foster family to another. By the age of 20, Will prefers to pick fights, drink heavily in pubs, and surround himself with friends who won't challenge him to find his more authentic self.

After being arrested, Will finds himself in prison. A mathematics professor recognises Will's extraordinary potential and bargains with the judge to release him, on the condition that Will meets regularly with a counsellor. Enter Robin Williams, playing Sean, the counsellor. Initially, Will tries to sabotage the first counselling sessions by provoking Sean. In one session, Will provocatively interprets a painting that Sean created of his late wife, suggesting that Sean has not come to terms with his wife's death. Though visibly upset, Sean does not walk away. Instead, Sean chooses vulnerability and honesty, sharing with Will the sadness of the death of his wife, and the pain of seeing her suffer through cancer and death.

When Will begins to open up, Sean repeatedly tells Will, "It's not your fault." At first, Will resists, but eventually, Will breaks down, allowing himself to feel the pain and trauma he has long buried. This moment marks the beginning of finding Will's more authentic self beyond the façade that everything is fine and normal. A loving friendship forms between Sean and Will. This relationship soon helps Will to see things differently and more completely.

Sean becomes a healing presence for Will, someone willing to sit with him in the brokenness and messiness of life. This kind of wholeness cannot come from individual effort alone, but from deep, authentic desire to connect. We, too, can be a healing presence for each other in stillness today, like Jesus, who hangs on the cross. Pause and imagine for a moment. Jesus' wounds are exposed to the wind and rain as you stand there watching.... Pause for one minute.....

Jesus' wounds become doorways to something more. In our own lives, our own wounds, and the wounds of others, can be doorways to our more authentic selves. If we come to terms with who we truly are, both wholeness and woundedness bubble to the surface, revealing something.

Are we willing to step into the messiness of our lives? In life, when faced with decisions, one must choose between the easy and the hard roads. Which road do we take? Sometimes, we prefer to sit on the sidelines, like a spectator in the grandstand, watching the game of life rather than playing it. In the grandstand, we can enjoy hot dogs and slushies, but we might avoid the sweat and struggle of playing on the field.

The Search for Authenticity

Do we search for authenticity? Are we players or spectators? How do we change from being a spectator to a player on the field?

For Christians, transformation takes many forms, but the core is the same: we must seek deeper truths in our journey. This may mean finding a counsellor, having a significant conversation, taking a new path, or experiencing an event that shakes us. It is precisely through our messiness and through the wounds in our lives that we begin to see something we have missed before. When we look through the holes in our hands, feet, and sides, as Jesus does, we discover that God is part of the road we take; God can transform these wounds. Though sometimes we hesitate out of fear or choose not to face the challenge before us.

Augustine of Hippo

In the 5th century CE, as a young man, Augustine was captivated by the pleasures of the world. He indulged in sensual desires, particularly in relationships with women, and gained public acclaim as a gifted teacher of rhetoric. His talents led him to prominent positions, even travelling to Rome and Milan to teach and speak. Despite his success and popularity, Augustine felt an aching emptiness within. The things he once thought would satisfy, pleasure, ambition, knowledge, and recognition, only deepened his restlessness. He came to realise that these pursuits, while alluring, could not fill the void in his soul. It was only through his eventual encounter with God that he experienced a radical change.

The turning point in Augustine's life came in a quiet garden in Milan in the year 386. Overwhelmed by the weight of his sins and his inability to commit fully to the life that he felt God was calling him to live, he collapsed into tears, a soul laid bare in anguish and desperation. In his book Confessions, he recounts this moment of crisis and breakthrough:

"I was asking myself these questions, weeping all the while with the most bitter sorrow in my heart, when all at once I heard the singing song voice of a child in a nearby house. Whether it was the voice of a boy or a girl, I cannot say, but again and again it repeated the refrain 'take it and read, take it and read'" (Augustine, p. 177, 1961).

Augustine took these words as a divine command. As if Jesus was speaking to him directly. Grasping a Bible, he opened it at random, and his eyes fell upon Romans 13:13–14:

"Let us live honourably as in the day... not in revelling and drunkenness... but put on the Lord Jesus Christ, and make no provision for the flesh, to gratify its desires."

In that instant, something shifted within Augustine. The words pierced his heart with clarity and power. His confusion melted away, and a profound sense of peace and purpose washed over him. It was not a surrender through fear or compulsion, but a surrender through grace, grace that illuminated his heart and opened the way to a new life anchored in Christ. From that moment, Augustine's restless searching gave way to a joyful belonging. Augustine later wrote, *"Our hearts are restless until they rest in You, O God."* This profound statement reflected not only a timeless spiritual truth but also his own deeply personal journey of inner struggle. Not that the struggle will disappear, but the way through becomes a different path with God with us. Resting in God requires trusting something beyond the self.

Francis of Assisi

Francis of Assisi also underwent a powerful change of heart, though his transformation was more gradual and marked by a series of painful awakenings. Born in 1181 into wealth and privilege, Francis was a carefree and spirited young man who loved parties, fine clothes, and the admiration of his peers. He sought glory and adventure, and in 1201, at the age of twenty, he rode off as a proud young knight to fight in a local skirmish against the neighbouring town of Perugia. His dreams were quickly shattered when he was captured in battle and thrown into a dark prison, where he languished for over a year.

Eventually, Francis was freed, but he remained a restless young man. Still clinging to the ideal of knighthood, he set out in 1205 to join the military campaign of the Fifth Crusade. Yet along the road to Spoleto, he fell gravely ill and, in a dream, received a divine message that would forever alter his course. He heard a voice ask, *"Francis, who do you serve, the servant or the Master?"* He replied, *"The Master."* The voice responded, *"Then why do you serve the servant?"* (Habig, p. 637, 1973)

This moment pierced his heart. It sparked a profound inner struggle that led Francis to question everything he once valued. He began giving away his wealth to the poor and embracing humility and simplicity. Outraged by his actions, Francis's father, Pietro di Bernardone, disowned his son. Stripped of all worldly possessions, Francis stood before the bishop of Assisi, renounced his inheritance, and walked away naked, clothed only in the love of God. From that point forward, Francis lived as a beggar, devoted to prayer, poverty, and serving the poor. His slow, unfolding conversion became a radiant witness to a radically Christ-centred life. Francis' road to authenticity had many twists, turns, and even defeats. Yet by surrendering his life more fully to Christ's way, Francis was able to discover more deeply who he truly was.

The Disciples

At the beginning of the Gospel story, Jesus did not seek out perfect people. People who were powerful, or the outwardly holy, were to be His closest followers. Jesus did not initially call the wealthy, the successful, or the respected Jewish leaders of his day. Instead, Jesus chooses the imperfect, flawed, ordinary people with complicated pasts and uncertain futures. Matthew was a tax collector, reviled by his fellow Jews for collaborating with the Roman occupiers and profiting from their oppression. Simon Peter, who would become the leader of the apostles, initially responded to Jesus' call with deep awareness of his unworthiness with *"Go away from me, Lord, for I am a sinful man"* (Luke 5:8, NRSV). Yet even after following Jesus closely, Peter would later deny Jesus three times during his darkest hour. The apostle Thomas, unable to believe in the resurrection without physical proof, became the symbol of doubt (John 20:24-29, NRSV). James and John, eager for status, asked for seats of honour in Jesus' kingdom, missing the call to servant leadership (Mark 10:35-45, NRSV). Simon the Zealot came from a background of political extremism, driven by a desire to violently overthrow Roman rule. And Judas Iscariot, one of the twelve, would ultimately betray Jesus for a handful of silver (Matthew 26:14-16, NRSV), triggering the events leading up to Jesus' death, later known as the Passion.

So why does Jesus choose such people, people full of imperfection, failure, and contradiction? Why call those who are anything but polished or perfect? Perhaps because Jesus sees what others cannot. He sees beyond failure and into the potential for something beyond what the eye can see. He chooses the imperfect not despite their flaws, but because through them, the power of God might be revealed.

Authentic Life

Can God become the doorway to a more authentic life? But where is God? We may not be able to see God. We may not even believe in God. In John 20:29, Jesus says to Thomas, *"Have you believed because you have seen me? Blessed are those who have not seen and yet have come to believe."* Peter writes, *"Although you have not seen him, you love him; and even though you do not see him now, you believe in him and rejoice with an indescribable and glorious joy, for you are receiving the outcome of your faith, the salvation of your souls."* (1 Peter 1:8–9). While St Paul writes, *"For we walk by faith, not by sight."* (2 Corinthians 5:7). It is as though not seeing or not believing is the better path to the journey of faith.

As a religious education high school teacher with twenty years of experience, I often tell my students, "It's okay to be an atheist" or "It's okay to be an agnostic." When I say this, I see their shoulders drop and their bodies relax. Suddenly, they feel permission to be themselves. This doesn't mean I fully agree with what they believe, or don't believe, but it opens the door for authentic dialogue. It allows honesty to enter the conversation. The old catechetical model, where I, as the teacher, simply tell students what to believe from the top down, no longer seems to work. In Australia, more than thirty percent of students attend Catholic schools, yet by the time they graduate, many walk away from the Church entirely. The factory model of producing committed Catholics year after year appears to be failing. Perhaps this points to a deeper truth, that faith cannot be mass-produced, but is best nurtured in spaces of authenticity, where smallness and genuine encounter matter more than numbers or efficiency. There is something more authentic in smallness. Like Jesus and the twelve apostles, there is something daring about taking a journey together in smaller numbers.

To become who we truly are, we must be willing to go on a journey beyond what we can see. Staying true to our values and what we hold dear requires us to stand firm in the face of opposition, not giving in to fleeting emotions that rise and fall. But what if our more authentic self doesn't fully align with who we are now? We must be willing to listen. Listen to another's voice. Like Mary, who listened to the angel's voice (Luke 1:26-38, NRSV) telling her something she did not expect, we must be open to different perspectives. It is only when we are willing to listen to what is unfamiliar, to stand in another's shoes, to walk alongside those from different social classes, that we can begin to become what we are not yet.

This is the paradox of being human. In the in-between places, where things may not make sense, we begin to discover a deeper truth about who we are. This truth is not something we invent; it is something we uncover by passing through the doorways of our lives and the relationships we choose to build. These relationships shape and influence who we are becoming.

Whether we choose to marry or remain single, our relationships profoundly shape who we are becoming. The people in our lives, our mothers, fathers, partners, and those in our close community, draw out who we are. We do not become ourselves in isolation; we need others to hold us up and support us. Additionally, how we relate to others influences our journey. Do we create mental barriers that prevent us from walking the path ahead? Or do life events, such as an accident or serious illness, tear down those barriers? These experiences can help us refocus and see life through a new lens, like taking off one pair of glasses and putting on another. As our perspective shifts, we are called to live a more authentic life.

In Mark 8:27–30, Jesus poses a critical question to His disciples:

Jesus went on with his disciples to the villages of Caesarea Philippi, and on the way he asked his disciples, "Who do people say that I am?"

And they answered him, "John the Baptist; and others, Elijah; and still others, one of the prophets."

He asked them, "But who do you say that I am?"

Peter answered him, "You are the Messiah."

And he sternly ordered them not to tell anyone about him.

The question, *"Who do you say that I am?"* is not just for the disciples; it is for each of us. Jesus does not leave this open to interpretation. In John 14:6, He says, *"I am the way, the truth, and the life."* Earlier in John's Gospel, He declares, *"I am the gate. Whoever enters by me will be saved, and will come in and go out and find pasture"* (John 10:9). The Jewish Pharisees at that time could not accept His words and, in their anger, picked up stones to stone Him. For us, too, living a more authentic life in Christ can be difficult. Those closest to us may resist or even place obstacles in our path, making it harder to step fully into the life to which we are called.

How can we know what we believe is true? There are several tests that can help us determine what we think, feel, and believe to be true.

First is accountability. Am I open to correction and support from other Christians? Proverbs says, *"Iron sharpens iron"* (27:17, NRSV), reminding us that an authentic life is lived in community, not isolation. Sharing honestly with people we trust can help us discern what is true from what is not. But we must be careful, some people are wise mentors and role models, while others may reinforce our false beliefs, twisting reality rather than seeking the truth. We need to be discerning about whom we listen to and consider the motivations of those who play a role in our lives. Are there people, perhaps a little older and wiser, with more lived experience, who have walked the path before us? Sometimes it takes time to find a good spiritual director or counsellor. Yet often, people within the wider Christian community can help point us in the right direction.

Second is the desire for God. Am I actively seeking God in my life? A growing desire for God often leads us to pray regularly in our day, to pause on a park bench and appreciate the present moment, or to simply be still in God's presence. But sometimes, we may not feel that desire. We may not enjoy praying, going to church, or seeking God in our regular moments of the day. This dryness can be a sign that something in our spiritual life needs attention. It may even be a sign that we're being called back to the right path. Paradoxically, when we don't desire God, it can actually be the starting place for encountering Him. As Matthew 7:7 reminds us: *"Ask, and it will be given you; search, and you will find; knock, and the door will be opened for you."* We must pray even when we don't feel like praying. Go to church even when we'd rather not. Change a nappy even when it doesn't feel like our turn. Volunteer to serve the poor when we would prefer to do our own thing. Read Scripture even when it seems boring. Take a long, quiet spiritual walk through our suburb or town when life feels like it's falling apart. Spiritual dryness is not a dead end; it's often an invitation. It can lead to a deeper awakening. In these moments, we may discover a new pathway to God, one we didn't know existed.

Third, fasting can deepen our desire for God. Do we give up the things our egos most crave? Rather than spending all of Saturday on an electronic device, we may decide not to touch it until sundown on Sunday. Giving up the things that we're crave about for a short time, like social media and playing computer games, helps expose the false self, the part of us that seeks comfort, control, and our own desires. Ultimately, our lives are not defined by what we can consume or control. As Jesus reminds us in Matthew 4:4, "One does not live by bread alone…" Fasting creates an interior space in our hearts for God. In that emptiness, we may find ourselves praying, "God, help me get through the pain, the suffering, and the absence of what I miss." Hunger reminds us of those in our world who go without, drawing us into deeper compassion and solidarity with the poor. In fasting, we become poor in spirit. As Augustine of Hippo once said, *"Fasting cleanses the soul, raises the mind, subjects the flesh to the spirit, renders the heart contrite and humble…"* (Augustine, Sermon 72, as cited in Schaff, 1887). When we are poor and poor in spirit, we are more able to attune ourselves to the love of God.

Fourth, what are we doing with our time? Do we watch violent or explicit movies that lead us down the wrong path? Do we play computer games that glorify killing or desensitise us to violence? We may not always realise that how we spend our time shapes who we are, and who we are becoming. Jesus says, *"See, I am sending you out like sheep into the midst of wolves; so be wise as serpents and innocent as doves"* (Matthew 10:16, NRSV). We must be discerning and choose wisely what we do. Are our actions aligned with our Christian values? Reading the Bible or other spiritual books, including this one, can help form our hearts and lead us to a more authentic life. How can we truly know Christ if we do not take time to learn about Him or encounter Him in our daily lives? Watching films or shows that reflect Christian values and virtues can subtly remind us of what we are called to. As the Psalmist writes, *"O Lord, you have searched me and known me. You know when I sit down and when I rise up; you discern my thoughts from far away... Where can I go from your spirit? Or where can I flee from your presence?"* (Psalm 139:1-2, 7). There must be consistency between our public and private lives. We cannot say one thing in certain settings or among certain people, and then act completely differently in the privacy of our homes. Integrity requires us to remove the masks we wear and stand firm in what we believe.

There are several layers in the process of becoming more authentic. In the film Shrek (Adamson, 2001), there is a memorable scene where Shrek explains to Donkey that ogres are like onions: *"Ogres are like onions... they have layers."* Donkey, confused, jokes that not everyone likes onions and suggests parfaits or French desserts instead. Yet the scene is meaningful; Shrek is trying to express that beneath his rough exterior lies depth. Layer upon layer, his identity is shaped by experience, pain, and guardedness. We, too, have layers, parts of ourselves that are hidden, ignored, or unacknowledged. As we draw closer to the life of God, we begin to uncover the layers in our own lives. In peeling back these layers, we don't just find our wounds and weaknesses; we also discover our sacred worth and our call to live fully in Christ.

If we truly believe that Jesus is the Messiah, the Son of God, should that belief not transform who we are? If Jesus is the Son of God, should that not change what we do and how we relate to one another? We become children of God not through our own achievements, but through what Jesus does in and through us by grace. A more authentic life draws us closer to God, and as we draw closer to God, we also come to know ourselves more deeply. Who we are called to be is revealed through the person of Jesus Christ. He is the way, the truth, and the life. Through Him, we come to see who we truly are, children of God.

Journal

Spend 20 minutes journaling about the following.

Choose ONE of the following questions to journal about

1. *In what ways can you suppress or hide your authentic self in order to fit in or feel accepted by others?*

2. *When have you encountered a moment, conversation, or relationship that helped peel back a layer of your identity, revealing something deeper beneath the surface?*

3. *What everyday habits or distractions stop you from living a more authentic life?*

4. *Have you ever experienced God's invitation through suffering, silence, or someone's love, like Sean in Good Will Hunting or Sam and Patrick in The Perks of Being a Wallflower. What did it reveal about who you truly are?*

5. *How has your belief in Jesus changed the way you live, love, and understand your identity as a child of God? Think of Augustine and Francis.*

6. *What parts of your life may be shaped more by cultural expectations than by who God is calling you to be at a deeper level?*

Journalling

Journalling

Journalling

Journalling

Prayer

Take a moment to pause.
  Close your eyes for two to three minutes.
  Become aware of your breathing.
  Breathe slowly.
  As you breathe in and as you breathe out.
  Afterwards, if it feels helpful, consider praying slowly this prayer in the days leading up to the next chapter.

Loving God,
You see beneath the surface of our lives and into the layers of who we truly are. In a world that pressures us to perform, to please, and to perfect, remind us that we are already enough in Your eyes, beloved, chosen, and called. Help us to strip away the false selves we've built and uncover the sacred worth You have placed within us. In our moments of doubt, may we remember that You are the way, the truth, and the life. Walk with us through the messy, beautiful journey of becoming more fully ourselves in You. Grant us the courage to listen, to grow, and to live with integrity and a deeper authenticity, open to the change that only Your love can bring. Amen.

Pause

Pause for one day or one week before going to the next chapter.

Allow the thoughts and ideas to sink in.

Reflect.

Ponder.

Journal.

Share with others.

Chapter Ten

Finding God

Reflection - Finding God in your breath...

"Your breath is like the rhythm of the ocean wave.
Take a moment now.
Focus on the rise and fall of your breath.

Pause for 1 minute.

Slowly breathe in all that is good.
Gently hold onto what you have.

Focus on this for 1 minute.

And then slowly breathe out.
Release and let go of what weighs you down.
Make a sound as you exhale, as though the tide is pulling the bad away.
Hand this over to God.

Focus on this for 1 minute.

Breathe in again.
Recognise the goodness, the gift of you from God.
Rest in God's presence.

Focus on this for 1 minute.

And slowly breathe out.
Release with sound, letting go of fear, of worry, of anything holding you down.
Hand this over to God.

Focus on this for 1 minute.

Your breath is like the ocean wave, always returning, always flowing back to God.

Repeat from the beginning until you are ready.

When you breathe out and make a gentle noise, such as humming, chanting, or even sighing, it helps activate the vagus nerve, which plays a key role in calming the body and mind. The vagus nerve is the main component of the parasympathetic nervous system, your body's "rest and digestive" system.

When you notice in your day that you are upset or you're struggling to deal with something emotionally, repeat this reflection "Finding God Breathe"... Make a conscious commitment to this breath exercise.

The Wind

The Hebrew word for wind is *"ruach"*. The first image of God in the Bible is that of wind. Ruach means breath or spirit. When you breathe, realise it is God's breath and not just your own. Ruach is closely linked to the idea of God's life-giving presence within humanity. In Genesis 2:7, God breathes into Adam's nostrils to give him life.

The story of Elijah

In the Old Testament of the Bible, the prophet Elijah fled to Mount Horeb because Queen Jezebel, the queen of the Kingdom of Samaria, sought to kill him (1 Kings 19:1-18, NRSV). Elijah took refuge in a cave. After some time, he came out, searching for God's presence.

While in this cave, first of all, there was a great and violent wind, but Elijah did not find God in the wind. So, he returned to the cave and waited.

Then Elijah came out a second time, still searching for God. This time, a powerful earthquake shook the ground, but God was not in it. Again, Elijah returned to the cave and waited.

He came out a third time, and a raging fire swept through the area, destroying all in its path. But God was not in the fire. So, Elijah returned once more to the cave and waited in silence.

Elijah waited. And he waited. And he waited.

Finally, he stepped out once more and stood still, listening. All he could sense was a gentle breeze, a soft whisper. And in that quiet stillness, Elijah realised that this was an experience of the true presence of God.

In our busy world, we often miss God. God is hidden, like the gentle breeze, subtle and easy to overlook. But sometimes, God also desires to stir things up. But at other times, the Holy Spirit is not a soft whisper; then God moves as a great, forceful wind, unpredictable and urgent.

Incarnation

God chose to enter humanity, not through grand announcements or blaring trumpets, but in one of the most backward and chaotic regions of the Roman Empire: Palestine around 4 BCE. This was a distant outpost on the empire's edge, home to a seemingly insignificant people. The Jewish people were a conquered people at the time.

And yet, God chose an unmarried teenage Jewish girl to bear His Son. In Judaism at that time, becoming pregnant outside of marriage could result in death by stoning. It is through this chaos, vulnerability, and risk that God entered our reality, reminding us that the divine is often found in unexpected places, through ordinary lives, and in the midst of turmoil.

The angel declared to Mary that *"the Holy Spirit will come upon you, and the power of the Most High will overshadow you"* (Luke 1:35, NRSV).

Mary

This image of the Holy Spirit hovering over Mary mirrors the Spirit hovering over the formless void in the Book of Genesis (1:2), bringing about a new creation in the world. This overshadowing is like the cloud that surrounded Mount Sinai when Moses ascended to meet God (Exodus 24:15-18). Mary would have been like any other person in 4BCE. When life presents itself, she cannot see the road ahead. Life was clouded in mystery. Like Mary, we cannot always see ahead or fully understand how the Holy Spirit will work in our own lives. Yet we are called to trust. Through a trust in faith, Mary becomes the new tabernacle (Luke 1:38), just as the Ark carried all life in the mythological story of Noah (Genesis 6-9), whilst the Ark of the Covenant, carrying the Ten Commandments, once travelled with Moses and guided the Israelites through the desert (Exodus 40:34-35). But now, the Ark is no longer made of wood, stone, or gold; it is made of human flesh, in the person of Jesus Christ, carried in the womb of Mary.

Holy Spirit

The Gospel relates that when Jesus had reached adulthood, he was baptised in the River Jordan. The Holy Spirit descends upon Him. As Matthew writes: *"When Jesus was baptised, immediately He went up from the water, and behold, the heavens were opened to Him, and He saw the Spirit of God descending like a dove and coming to rest on Him"* (Matthew 3:16-17, NRSV).

Every time a person experiences the Holy Spirit, it brings about a significant change in their life. While we cannot see the Spirit, we can often see its effects. As Origen beautifully puts it, the Spirit does not leave us where we are, but constantly moves us into deeper intimacy with God (Origen, 1966, II.7.2).

The Spirit works in ways that are deeply personal, a divine signature unique to each life. It can be difficult to recognise the Holy Spirit's presence as the Spirit relates to us through our own lives.

As John writes, *"The wind blows where it wishes, and you hear its sound, but you do not know where it comes from or where it is going"* (John 3:8,

NRSV). So, it is with the Spirit, subtle, mysterious, yet always inviting us into new life.

We are called to recognise how God works through our own lives. Through the ups and the downs. In ordinary moments, does the Spirit flow through us? To recognise its effects and allow the Spirit to more fully be part of our lives, we must first empty ourselves of the things that block us from fully receiving God's love. As Richard Rohr (2015) suggests, Modern Christianity has become a religion of addition rather than transformation through subtraction. As. Christians, we often focus on what we are not doing. Maybe going to church on Sunday or praying every day with our family. Maybe the answer is not adding more things to our daily routines. Maybe the answer is to step back from business as usual, pause for a while, and let the absence of something shape our reality.

Too often, we can focus on external actions, following more rules, believing specific truths, and behaving in a certain way. But that's the paradox: we don't need to do anything to earn God's love. God is ultimately the one who acts.

Remember, God existed before we were born and will exist after we die. God works before us, after us, and even within us now. God's Spirit was at work long before human beings were created. The Australian continent is often described as the land of the Holy Spirit, seen as a place where the Spirit dwells. The Spirit lives in the land. For Australian Aboriginal people, this is not just an idea or concept, but something that actively shapes and moulds the land on which we walk. In a sense, the land is alive with the Spirit's presence. However, through Western eyes, we often fail to see the deeper reality of God's Spirit dwelling in the land and, by extension, in our lives.

Judas

In the contemporary TV series, The Chosen (Jenkins, 2017), there is a powerful imagined scene in Season 5 in which Jesus sits privately with Judas before Judas betrays Jesus, for a heated conversation. Jesus challenges Judas to think differently. This is an apocryphal moment, thus not found in the Bible, but it offers insight into what might have motivated Judas to betray Jesus.

In the scene, Judas expresses a series of expectations, hoping that Jesus will physically overthrow the Roman rule and restore the Kingdom of David in a political and material sense. Judas essentially issues an ultimatum to Jesus, suggesting that events are teetering on a knife's edge and warning that things will become disastrous, we can infer violent, if Jesus does not act according to his expectations.

Jesus asks Judas, *"You have a choice to make, Judas. Who do you belong to? Who has your heart?"*

Judas quietly responds, *"You have it."*

At times, we too can act like Judas. In one moment, we can sincerely say, *"You have my heart"*, but in the next, our actions reveal the opposite. We begin to craft our own plans, imagining various schemes and strategies to move forward. But this is not faith; it is reliance on our own human designs, rather than trust in something more.

If we truly love God, shouldn't that love challenge us to redirect the course of our lives? We should learn to let go. We must discover how subtraction works, to step back, reflect, and make room for something new. Are we willing to surrender control and release what is holding us back from fully entering into the love of God?

The Shack

In the film *"The Shack"* (Hazeldine, 2017), a loving father named Mack faces unimaginable tragedy when his young daughter is brutally abducted and murdered during a family camping trip. Consumed by grief, rage, sorrow, helplessness, and guilt, Mack finds himself unable to reconcile the horror of what has happened. His heart harbours a desire for vengeance against the man responsible. In a pivotal moment, Mack receives an invitation to return to the very shack where his daughter's life was taken, a place now steeped in trauma. There, he encounters three mysterious and divine figures: Papa, God the Father, portrayed as a compassionate, nurturing mother; Jesus, who gently guides Mack toward healing; and Sarayu, the Holy Spirit, who helps him confront his bitterness and teaches him the power of letting go. Throughout the encounter, Mack wrestles with deep emotional pain, the raw weight of resentment, and especially with his anger toward God. He demands answers, questioning how a loving God could allow such a terrible thing to happen. Eventually, Mack opens up to the possibility of forgiveness, but only after a great internal struggle.

Forgiveness

Each of us is called to forgive. Forgiveness is one of the essential keys that can change our world. You may feel that you don't need forgiveness, but someone else, a person, a group, or even a nation, might. Our hearts can be filled with greed, hurt, pain, obstacles, and a reluctance to let go. God calls us to let go. Each day, speak the words: "I forgive…" The world will begin to change, one heart at a time. In our world today, there is often no room for forgiveness. We fail to make room in our hearts for that which we would rather avoid. We might think to ourselves, "I don't need God to forgive sins, I haven't done anything wrong." But have we missed something here? Jesus doesn't just encourage us to seek God's forgiveness, but rather, He calls us, you and me, to forgive each other. This is not just about God, but also about how we treat each other.

We may feel we do not need God's forgiveness. But forgiveness is the doorway to something more. The act of forgiveness requires us to step into the broken and uncomfortable parts of our lives. It often defies logic and exceeds what seems possible. To move beyond the psychological patterns or complexes that shape our lives. Yet, forgiveness opens us to a deep and transformative love, a love that could not have existed before. A love that draws us closer to God. Through love we find God.

An Amish story of forgiveness

On October 6, 2006, a gunman named Charles Roberts entered a one-room Amish schoolhouse in Lancaster County, Pennsylvania, and took ten girls hostage. Tragically, he shot each of them; five girls died, and the other five suffered critical injuries. Roberts, a local milk truck driver with no prior criminal record, had been struggling with deep personal grief and anger, particularly over the death of his infant daughter years earlier. He left suicide notes for his wife, revealing his inner turmoil and despair.

Incredibly, in the face of this horrific tragedy, the Amish leaders publicly forgave Charles Roberts, the man who killed their daughters. Within a day, members of the Amish community visited Roberts' widow and extended their forgiveness to her. One Amish man even held Roberts' father in his arms to comfort him. Around 30 Amish individuals attended Roberts' funeral. In response, his widow, Marie Roberts, wrote an open letter to her Amish neighbours, expressing deep gratitude for their forgiveness, grace, and mercy.

She wrote, *"Your love for family has helped provide the healing we desperately need"* (Kraybill, 2007).

The story of Kim Phuc Phan Thi

On one fateful day, June 8, 1972, a young girl named Kim Phuc Phan Thi was taking shelter in a Cao Dai temple with her village in Vietnam during the Vietnam civil war. Tragically, South Vietnamese planes dropped napalm bombs near the temple. The explosion was so intense that the young Kim's clothes were burned off, and she was soon seen running naked down the road, badly burned and in excruciating pain. An American photographer captured the haunting image of her terrified and injured body fleeing for her life, a photo that would become iconic around the world. Kim was rushed to Saigon hospital, where doctors did not expect Kim to survive. She had burns on over thirty percent of her body and required seventeen surgeries to recover. She survived. Later, Kim reflected on that.

"Although the burns on my body were being treated, I had not treated the wounds I wore in my heart... Just like napalm, anger and bitterness consumed me and threatened to burn up my soul" (Phan Thi,2017).

Kim soon discovered Christianity. A radical change took over. She began praying one by one for each man who had hurt her so badly. Eventually, in 1996, 24 years after the event, I met the man responsible for the attack in 1972 and offered forgiveness.

"I was full of hatred, anger, bitterness, and darkness. I felt like I was living in hell. But one day, I knew I had to change, I had to learn to forgive.

If I let the hatred consume me, I would never be free.

The pain from the burns will always remain, but my heart is no longer on fire" (Phan Thi,2017).

The Abbey

In the ABC TV documentary series The Abbey (Sidwell, 2007), Sister Hilda Scott guided five Australian women through 33 days of life in a Benedictine monastery, where they experienced the challenges of monastic life, including long periods of silence, regular prayer, manual labour, and community life.

During this short time of stillness and communal living, personal and emotional traumas begin to surface in each of the women in different ways. They were given permission to be themselves in a safe place. The women spoke more openly to Sister Hilda, sharing many of the hurts and pains they had carried for years. Sister Hilda listened with a loving, compassionate ear and the warmth of a mother's heart.

In one scene, she illustrates the emotional burdens we carry by bringing a heavy backpack. During the meeting, Sister Hilda opened the backpack, revealing large stones inside. Each stone, she explains, represented the hurts, wounds, and sins we carry day by day, burdens that weigh us down and prevent us from living fully. She encourages the women to recognize these stones, become aware of them, and begin letting them go through prayer and forgiveness. But this journey is not meant to be walked alone. Sister Hilda emphasised that we need one another. And more importantly, we need the Holy Spirit to move through our lives, lighten our load, and reshape our hearts. As our hearts break open, they may allow us to find God through the deeper realities of our lives.

A loving father

In all our seeking, struggling, and surrendering, the image that emerges most powerfully is that of a loving Father, the God who waits at the end of the road, arms open, ready to embrace us even when we have wandered far. Just as the father in the parable of the Prodigal Son (Luke 15:11-32) who runs to meet his child, so too does God long to draw near to us, not with condemnation, but with mercy, joy, and love of a father.

Jesus often referred to God as *"Abba,"* an Aramaic word that carries the tender intimacy of "Dad" or "Daddy." It is not the title of a distant deity, but the cry of trust from a child who knows they are deeply loved. This name, Abba, is not simply theological; it is deeply personal and intimate. It reminds us that we are not alone in our pain, our confusion, or our longing. Whether we are letting go of anger, offering forgiveness, or standing still in the silence waiting for the Spirit's whisper, God is near us. God is not a far-off, cruel judge, but our Abba, the One who breathes life into us, walks beside us through the fire, weeps when we suffer, and celebrates when we return. And in calling God Abba, we discover again the very heart of the Christian flame: we are known, we are loved, and we are home.

As we face the turbulent moments of our lives. As we discover the trauma that has shaped our history. As we deal with the problems of our modern day, we need only breathe. Through time, find a way to allow God to breathe through your life.

Take a moment to sit with this.

You may need to start this chapter again, as we did the breathing exercise at the beginning.

Journal

Spend 20 minutes journaling about the following.

Choose ONE of the following questions to journal about

1. *What does the wind and our breath teach us about God's presence in our daily lives,?*

2. *How does the story of Elijah remind us to look for God not in dramatic signs, but in stillness and silence?*

3. *Why do you think God chose to enter the world in such an unexpected way, through Mary, in an obscure corner of the Roman Empire? What does this tell us about how God works in our lives?*

4. *How does the idea of letting go of control, ego, our desires, or expectations help us make space for the Holy Spirit? Can you think of something in your life you need to let go of to draw closer to God?*

5. *Why is forgiveness such an important part of Christian life? Is there someone in your life you are being invited to forgive? What might happen if you did? Or maybe, you need to forgive that part of you that has kept you from more fully loving.*

6. *What can we learn from the stories of Judas, Mack in The Shack, the Amish community, and Kim Phuc in our own lives?*

Journalling

Journalling

Journalling

Journalling

Prayer

Take a moment to pause.
  Close your eyes for two to three minutes.
  Become aware of your breathing.
  Breathe slowly.
  As you breathe in and as you breathe out.
  Afterwards, if it feels helpful, consider praying slowly this prayer in the days leading up to the next chapter.

Loving Abba, our Father,
You are the breath that gives us life, the whisper in the silence, and the fire that stirs our hearts toward love. Like Elijah in the cave and Mary carrying the Word made flesh, help us to trust in Your presence even when it is hidden or unexpected. Teach us to let go of pain, fear, resentment, and to make space for Your Holy Spirit to dwell within us. Following the way of Jesus, may we find the courage to forgive, to heal, and to live with hearts open to grace. Remind us that we are never alone, that You walk with us always as a tender and merciful Father, our Abba, calling us home. Amen.

Pause

Pause for one day or one week before going to the next chapter.

    Allow the thoughts and ideas to sink in.

    Reflect.

    Ponder.

    Journal.

    Share with others.

Chapter Eleven

Through community we ignite the Christian flame

Reflection - We only know human beings

"*In the dead of night, they came.*
Rain was falling all around.
We were asleep in our beds,
While the Nazis swept through our country,
Rampaging, taking people away.

I was a small child.
Then,

A thunderous knock at our door.
I didn't see them.
My mother whispered,
"Stay in your bed."
It was 1 a.m.
Still, they banged.

My father went downstairs.
And opened our screeching door.
A voice -sharp, -violent -shouted:
"You are hiding the Jews!"

Echoes of fear shook our house.
My father stood firm.
He replied calmly,
"We do not know what a Jew is. We only know human beings."

Again, the man demanded,
"Where are they? The Jews?"
And again, my father spoke,
His voice unwavering:
"We do not know what a Jew is. We only know human beings."

The man paused.
Then piercingly declared,
"Come with us." (The author)

Throughout human history, there have been countless stories of people responding to human need. When others suffer, there may be something within us that reaches out to change this reality. Though when we see constant images on the television or social media, we can become desensitised. But when we draw closer to people and see them face to face, they are no longer strangers; over time, they might become friends, or even feel like family. Our intimacy with another person in a close-knit community allows us to respond in ways we might not when they are mere strangers. Here are some stories that show how, in the community, people were called to change and respond.

Le Chambon-sur-Lignon

The small country town of Le Chambon-sur-Lignon, located in the remote region of south-eastern France, held a strong Protestant Christian tradition. The townspeople had a long history of persecution, dating back to the 16th and 17th centuries when Protestantism was outlawed in France. During World War II, when the Nazis invaded, their pastor, André Trocmé, delivered a powerful sermon. He stated:

"We shall resist whenever our adversaries demand that we act against our conscience. We do not know what a Jew is. We only know human beings." (Hallie, 1979).

Le Chambon-sur-Lignon was able to shelter between 3,000 to 5,000 Jewish refugees between 1942 and 1944 in Nazi occupied France.

The Story of Father Damien

In 1873, Father Damien De Veuster volunteered to serve at a leper colony on Molokai, one of the outer islands of Hawaii (Bouchareb & Troch, 1999). At the time, leprosy was widespread, and the government had exiled many people with the disease to a remote island. When Father Damien arrived, he found the community in chaos, people were living in squalor, struggling to survive, and many Hawaiians had abandoned their Christian values, treating one another like animals with disrespect and even abuse.

Father Damien immediately began to care for the people, tending to the sick and wounded, and building homes and shelters. But his mission extended beyond physical care; he also addressed their emotional and spiritual needs. He celebrated church services, heard confessions, and administered sacraments, including baptisms. He referred to those in the colony as "my brothers and my sisters," breaking down the stigma and social isolation associated with leprosy.

Over time, the community began to change. Hearts softened, and people began treating one another with dignity and respect. Despite initial resistance from some, Father Damien gradually won them over through his compassion and selfless service. In 1885, Damien himself contracted leprosy, and he died in 1889, having given his life fully to the people he served.

The Blind Side

On a cold, wintry night in 2002 in Memphis, Tennessee, a teenage boy named Michael, known to most as *"Big Mike",* walked alone through the rain (Hancock, 2009). He was a large, quiet teenager, carrying the weight of a difficult past. Homeless and nearly invisible to the world around him, Michael had grown up in deep poverty, his life shaped by instability and a mother battling drug addiction.

Then something changed. From the warmth of her car, Leigh Anne Tuohy spotted Michael trudging down the street, shivering in the cold winter weather with nowhere to go. Something stirred in Leigh to do something. She didn't know Mike's story, but she could see his suffering. Moved by something deep within, she stepped out of her car, walking slowly towards Mike. Gently saying, "Mike. Mike. Do you want to come home with us?"

Mike agreed. Got into the car. Warmth surrounded them. Soon, a comfortable bed to sleep on and the safety of a home.

What began as a simple act of kindness blossomed into something much, much more. Leigh Anne and her family offered Michael not just a bed and warm clothes, but a place to belong. A room of his own. A seat at their table. And, most importantly, a family that believed in him.

In time, Michael's life began to change. Surrounded by love, structure, and encouragement, he discovered not only his strength on the football field but also his worth as a person. The story of The Blind Side, based on true events, reminds us how one moment of generosity can open the door to a whole new life.

The COVID Crisis

It appears that the COVID crisis exposed our vulnerability and revealed the fallacy of individualism as the organising principle of Western society (Long, 2021). It shattered the myth of self-sufficiency, which has long justified rampant inequality and weakened the bonds that hold our communities together. Instead, the COVID pandemic highlighted our mutual dependency, our interconnectedness, and our shared fragility. In essence, we need each other.

The selflessness of doctors, nurses, healthcare workers, and others who maintained essential services during the lockdown crisis stands as a powerful reminder: our lives are a gift for each other. We grow not by preserving ourselves, but by giving of ourselves, not in isolation, but by losing ourselves in service to others, and we find the Christian flame.

Human Design

The human person is created with relationship in mind. It is through community that we discover a deeper calling, both as Christians and as human beings. Our relationships shape who we are, and we come more fully alive when we begin to care for one another.

Saint Augustine once wrote:

"God created us so that we might exist and live. But this is not enough: we must also live together in friendship. Two things are essential in this world: life and friendship. Both must be highly prized and not undervalued. For life and friendship are nature's gifts" (Saint Augustine, Sermon 299D).

The Trinity

Who we are reflects the very nature of God. Christians believe that God is a community of persons, as revealed in the Holy Trinity. The Father sends the Son; the Son lives to do the Father's will through word, deed, and self-giving love, ultimately offering His life back to the Father. The Holy Spirit is poured out from the Father and the Son, each lives for the other in perfect communion.

We are chosen to participate in this divine community. The Trinity is not some distant or abstract idea; it is a reality, binding all of life together in an eternal relationship of love. We, too, are designed for this kind of relational living with God and with each other.

However, when something threatens this sacred relationship, such as injustice toward our fellow human beings, we are drawn to respond. This response awakens something deep within us: our identity as instruments of God's mercy in the world today.

And yet, there is fear. In modern society, our egos often resist the vulnerability and cost that true community demands. We may fear letting go of control or self-preservation. But community calls us to more, to give of ourselves, to love more deeply, and to reflect the life of the Trinity through how we share and relate to each other.

Pentecost

After Jesus ascended to the Father (Acts 1:9), the disciples once again gathered together, locked in one place. Jesus had instructed them to stay there and wait for the promise of the Father (Acts 1:4), saying, *"You will be baptized with the Holy Spirit."* We should realize that this instruction was not meant only for the apostles 2,000 years ago; it is meant for us today. Jesus calls us to gather as a family, as a community, so that the Holy Spirit may be poured out upon us. But before that happened, the apostles prayed together in one place.

We are invited to pray together, but at times resist. Are we afraid? Our fears can prevent us from gathering with others. We tell ourselves a thousand reasons why we shouldn't come together. We make excuses for not going to church. Yet the word *"ekklesia"* literally means *"gathering of those who are called out"*. Jesus calls us to gather, saying, *"Where two or three are gathered in my name, I am there among them"* (Matthew 18:20).

In the Book of Acts, we read:

"When the day of Pentecost came, they were all together in one place. Suddenly from heaven there came a sound like the rush of a violent wind, and it filled the entire house where they were sitting" (Acts 2:1–2, NRSV).

The Holy Spirit was poured out as the disciples and Mary gathered as a Christian community. For followers of Jesus, gathering is essential; it creates space for the Spirit of God to descend more fully upon each person. Think of a wood fire. A single hot coal can burn, but when many coals are brought together, the fire burns brighter and stronger. So, it is with us; our faith is rekindled and strengthened in community.

The Prophet Isaiah writes.

"See, I have refined you, though not as silver; I have tested you in the furnace of affliction" (48:10, NRSV)

The fire that God speaks of is displayed in how we live. But how do we bring the Spirit of God to life within us? In both the ups and the downs, do we call upon the Holy Spirit to be present and active in our journey? It is often in the moments when we are burned, when we suffer, struggle, or are tested, that our faith is refined. Like gold, we are purified through the fire. The trials we face can deepen our reliance on God and shape us into who we are meant to become.

After the apostles received the Holy Spirit, that same Spirit continued to be poured out. Later, in cities like Ephesus and throughout Greece, the Book of Acts records:

"When Paul placed his hands on them, the Holy Spirit came on them, and they spoke in tongues and prophesied" (Acts 19:6, NRSV).

The Church is called to be born anew in our time, not only in the past, but in the present moment. John writes

"Whoever believes in me, as Scripture has said, rivers of living water will flow from them" (7:38-39, NRSV).

The prophet Ezekiel also proclaims God's promise:

"I will give you a new heart and put a new spirit in you. I will remove from you your heart of stone and give you a heart of flesh. And I will put my Spirit in you and move you to follow my decrees and be careful to keep my laws" (36:26–27, NRSV).

God's Spirit can actively transform us through the experience of community. This change is the love of God entering into us. Like the Trinity, we are guided to pour out that love for the sake of others. God's Spirit is overflowing. We are called to do the same to pour out God's love, and we are sent to bring that Good News into the world (see Matthew 28:16–20).

Our families and communities are not the end in themselves; they must always reach toward the margins, toward those who are forgotten or excluded. Like Leigh in the Blind Side with Mike, or André Trocmé in war-torn France, or Father Damien in Molokai, so we are urged to do the same in our world today. As Jesus read from the scroll of the prophet Isaiah:

"The Spirit of the Lord is upon me, because he has anointed me to bring good news to the poor" (Luke 4:18, NRSV).

Jesus fulfilled this mission, and we are challenged to follow Him in the same way.

A beginning.....

Before we can respond, we need to get to know people. Each of us comes from different backgrounds and has different levels of experience, connection to the community, and faith. It takes time for the barriers that separate us to come down, and we feel more comfortable responding with compassion and mercy. Connection beyond what is expected is where the story begins.

In John's Gospel, Jesus begins His ministry by going beyond the boundaries of His Jewish community. He travels to a region called Samaria, which lay between Galilee in the north and Judea in the south, a place many Jews of first-century Palestine avoided. Due to deep historical and racial tensions, most Jewish travellers preferred to take a longer route around Samaria to avoid contact with the Samaritan people. But Jesus chose to go straight through Samaria.

Jesus arrived alone at Jacob's well in the heat of the day, where He met a Samaritan woman, an encounter that would have been highly controversial at that time. Jesus asks her, *"Give me a drink."* Surprised, she responds, *"How is it that you, a Jew, ask a drink of me, a woman of Samaria? Jews do not share things in common with Samaritans"* (John 4:9, NRSV).

As their conversation unfolded, we learn that the woman had had several husbands, a fact that likely contributed to her social isolation. She had come to the well at noon, avoiding the early morning hours when other women would typically gather. But Jesus came to her at the unusual hour she was there, but Jesus did not judge her. He listened. When she exclaims, *"I see you are a prophet,"* it reflects both her anguish and her recognition that Jesus sees her truly at a deeper level.

At that time, prophets were known for calling people to justice and holding other people accountable. Yet Jesus daringly declares to her, "I am the Messiah." This moment is extraordinary. Despite her past, her gender, and the cultural barriers between them, Jesus treats her with incredible dignity, respect, and inclusion. Moved by this encounter, the woman begins to have new insights. Her heart changes because of how Jesus treats her. Jesus sees her as a woman with value and dignity. Though she had been judged and dismissed by others, Jesus chose her, an outcast, to be the first person to whom He began His good news as the Messiah. When the disciples return, they are shocked. *"Why are you speaking to her?"* they ask. Jesus had broken through deeply ingrained cultural and religious norms in her hour of need. In social isolation. She had felt worthless, yet Jesus offered her inherent worth through his recognition, inclusion, and relationship with her.

For us today, it is often the people right in front of us to whom we are called to be bearers of the Good News. Each person's needs will vary, so we must learn to tune in to those around us. But we are not simply meant to connect or get along with those within our circle of safety, our close friends, or those who make us feel comfortable.

Circles of Trust

Jesus calls us to look beyond our circles of trust, toward the excluded, the outcast, and even the people who get on our nerves. These may be individuals in our own families, or those we avoid speaking to at school or work. They may even be the stranger on the street. And yet, it is precisely there, in those often-uncomfortable places, that we are invited to bring His presence.

At Cana, in John Chapter 2, Mary and Jesus are invited to a wedding feast. Towards the end of the wedding, Mary notices that the wine has run out, she turns to Jesus and asks Him to respond. We, too, are called to do what Mary did: to notice the needs of others and to respond. But Mary did not act alone. She brought the need to Jesus.

Today, likewise, we are invited to respond by recognising the needs around us and bringing these needs to Jesus by making time for prayer, by changing our willingness to help, and by taking practical actions that pour out Christ's good news.

To enter more fully into the life of the Christian community, we need others, those closer to the community, to help draw us in. Like the story of the Good Shepherd at the gate (John 10:1–10), who stands at the door calling His sheep by name, we are called to be that presence for others. Similarly, in the story of Zacchaeus, Jesus notices a man on the margins, perched in a tree outside the crowd. Jesus calls him down, observes his inherent worth and goodness, and honours him as someone he cares about. In the same way, we are inspired to be like the Good Shepherd, attentive, welcoming, and ready to draw others into the heart of our family and friends' community. We are led to go beyond what is expected in the world around us.

Hospitality

The word hospitality comes from the Latin *"hospes"*, which originally meant *"stranger"* or *"foreigner,"* and later evolved to mean *"host"* or *"guest."* When Jesus is baptised by John the Baptist in the River Jordan, the Holy Spirit descends upon Him. But we can miss the fact that shortly afterwards, Jesus begins His ministry. The Holy Spirit pushes Him beyond His circle of safety into places He had not yet travelled. When Mary conceived Jesus, the Holy Spirit overshadowed her (Luke 1:35), and soon after, Mary set out to visit her cousin Elizabeth. Mary extends hospitality to her cousin who is in need beyond what is expected. The Holy Spirit calls us to move. A test of whether the Spirit is active in our lives is this: Are we using the gifts God has given us to help others in need? Have we been called to step beyond what is familiar and comfortable? If the answer is no, then perhaps we need to reflect often and invite the Holy Spirit to become more active in our lives, to stir us up, and to gather together with others like a family, as a community, and pray and be sent out. But the question is, "Where are we called to go?"

Pay it Forward

This rich concept of hospitality is beautifully conveyed in the film *"Pay It Forward"* (Leder, 2000). In the story, a Social Studies teacher named Eugene gives his class an assignment: *"Think of an idea to change the world and put it into action."* One student, Trevor, comes up with the idea of helping people in a significant and profound way. His model is simple: help one person in a profound and personal way, and in return, that person must go on to help three others, thus creating a ripple effect of kindness.

Trevor begins by helping a homeless man with food and shelter. He then tries to repair his mother's love life, and later helps his teacher, Eugene, find friendship and healing. Each of these individuals, in turn, is inspired to help others. Without giving away the ending. The film powerfully illustrates how one boy's act of hospitality and compassion inspires a movement that touches the lives of hundreds.

But the ripple effect we are invited to create is not something we need to do alone. Jesus tells us, *"I am the vine, and you are the branches"* (John 15:5). We can call upon the presence and inspiration of Jesus and the Gospel to guide us in carrying things forward. The Gospel not only provides us with a framework for sharing Jesus' Good News, but also points us to inspirational people throughout history who have embodied this same call, giving us a unique window into how to live out the Gospel message.

Catherine McAuley

In the early 1820s, Catherine McAuley sought to care for the poor on the streets of Dublin. Drawing on her personal wealth, she reached out to support the homeless and those in need. Catherine's inspiration came from her own upbringing, particularly the example of her father, who regularly cared for the poor, and later the Callaghan family, who encouraged her to read the Bible and supported her desire to care for them in their old age. Catherine established a house on Baggot Street, Dublin, where she provided care for the poor, offered free education to children whose families could not afford it, and equipped girls with practical skills such as sewing and cooking to foster their self-sufficiency. Other women soon joined Catherine in her mission, stepping out onto the streets at a time when religious women typically stayed safely behind monastic walls. Catherine and her companions entered the community to care for the sick and the dying, and they established the religious community of the Sisters of Mercy.

Amid all this work, Catherine also showed deep care for her fellow sisters, often encouraging them to pause, *"have a cup of tea,"* pray, and read Scripture. While hospitality and compassion were extended to those around her, Catherine recognized the importance of nurturing both physical and spiritual well-being, understanding that attending to their own needs enabled the Mercy Sisters to continue the vital work to which they were called.

We are often moved inwardly when someone we do not expect shows us care, extends hospitality, and invites us to sit at their table. What makes us more human is our desire to care for others in ways that they do not anticipate. When a mother holds her baby for the first time, the baby's eyes may open, but they are not yet able to focus; their vision is still developing. Yet, there is a deeper, physical connection that binds mother and child, something beyond words, calling both to change and grow into something that did not exist before: a mother and her child. It is like the scent of new daffodils on a spring morning, awakening a love that overflows with the essence of something divine. This love does not act selfishly; it radiates outward like the sun, calling forth new life and enabling the community around it to bloom.

Journal

Spend some time, maybe 20 minutes, journaling about the following.

Choose ONE of the following questions to journal about

1. *When have I witnessed or received unexpected hospitality that deeply affected me?*

2. *How do I respond when I am called to step beyond my comfort zone to help someone in need?*

3. *In what ways am I being invited to see others not as labels or categories, but simply as human beings?*

4. *What fears hold me back from gathering in community or offering myself in service?*

5. *How can I better use the gifts the Holy Spirit has given me to bring life and hope to others?*

6. *Who in my life today might be waiting for someone to notice them, listen to them, and invite them in?*

Journalling

Journalling

Journalling

Journalling

Prayer

Take a moment to pause.
　Close your eyes for two to three minutes.
　Become aware of your breathing.
　Breathe slowly.
　As you breathe in and as you breathe out.
　Afterwards, if it feels helpful, consider praying slowly this prayer in the days leading up to the next chapter.

Loving God,
You created us for a relationship, with You and with one another. You call us to move beyond comfort, beyond fear, and beyond labels, to see every person as Your beloved. Stir in us the courage of prophets, the tenderness of saints, and the boldness of the Spirit poured out at Pentecost. May we, like Jesus, walk toward the margins, listen to the unheard, and offer hospitality that transforms hearts. Fill us with Your love that overflows, radiating like sunlight, awakening new life, and building communities rooted in justice, hospitality, mercy, and hope. Amen.

Pause

Pause for one day or one week before going to the next chapter.

    Allow the thoughts and ideas to sink in.

    Reflect.

    Ponder.

    Journal.

    Share with others.

Chapter Twelve

Discovering a life of simplicity

Reflection - To sit on the rock

"*I leave the car at the roadside.*
  I leave the systems and pressures behind.
I walk down the path covered by the trees.
Gravel crunching under my feet.
The rich scent of eucalyptus trees fills my nostrils.
Birds fly in the distance.
As I descend the path of discovery, I feel alone.
No one is here.
But somehow, I am connected,

beyond the wilderness of my life". (The author)

We have been asleep at the wheel. In recent Christian history, we have ignored our role of stopping. We need to get out of our cars and our busyness and take a long walk in the bushlands, forests, and wilderness near our homes.

The Way

At the beginning of the film The Way (Estevez, 2010), Tom, an eye doctor, is busily managing his practice and playing golf. He has little time for family or anything else. Suddenly, Tom receives a phone call. A police officer in France calls him to inform Tom that his son Daniel has died unexpectedly. Shocked by the news, Tom cancels his work commitments and golfing game and flies to the South of France.

Many weeks later, when Tom arrived in France to identify Daniel's body and recover Daniel's personal belongings, including his backpack, he took it to his hotel and began unpacking it. Items for Daniel's journey gradually emerged. A map. A compass. A flashlight. Then Tom discovers a small photo album containing pictures of himself. Seeing his own photo that Daniel, his only son, is carrying in his personal belongings, Tom breaks down in tears, overwhelmed by the depth of his loss. Suddenly, Tom recalls another conversation with Daniel, who declared, *"I'm not finishing my doctorate. Dad, when was the last time you travelled? I don't mean for business; I mean before Mum got sick."* This flashback profoundly affected Tom. In his sadness and grief over his son's death, this changes Tom. Earlier, Tom discovered Daniel wanted to complete the 800-kilometre walk from the south of France across the top of Spain. The El Camino walk. Suddenly, Tom decides to complete that walk himself.

We often don't realise, as Tom does, what is most important to us until we lose it. When we lose what is precious to us, or when things seem to fall apart, then we begin to realise what truly matters. This process gives us a clearer focus. Often, these things are the people we love and the beautiful moments we share with them. Simplicity isn't about simple material things or being simple-minded. Living a life of simplicity means tapping into what truly matters to us.

Camping

In Australia, families often have a tradition of going camping for holidays. Holidays can be very expensive, making camping with a simple nylon tent and a few essentials one of the more affordable options. Packing for camping requires careful planning. Knowing exactly what to bring and ensuring it fits into your bag or car can be hard. Determining what is essential is key, as most belongings from home are left behind.

Upon arrival at a campsite, setting up quickly becomes crucial, ideally during a dry period to avoid rain or thunderstorms. However, sometimes a thunderstorm may strike just when you want to set up your tent, making the process stressful as you try to pitch it while it is being blown away by strong winds. Despite this, something interesting can happen in these challenging moments. You might realise that, despite the rain and thunder, you can get through it. Once, when my family first pitched a tent during a thunderstorm, I literally experienced a panic attack. My heart raced. My thoughts were quite negative. Looking back and reflecting later, well after this event, I understood that my family and I would be fine. I visualised myself and my family pitching a tent in a storm. So, the next time my family pitched a tent in similar conditions, I was prepared not only physically, but emotionally, and some might even say spiritually.

After a few days of camping, you may not need most of the things that you have at home. There is something quite liberating in becoming aware that we truly require very little. Marie Kondo's hit series "Tidying Up with Marie Kondo" (Kondo, 2019) has rekindled people's desire to live more simply. The central principle of her simplicity approach involves decluttering by holding each item and asking, "Does this spark joy?" Marie believes that each item should be treated with respect. The goal is not simply to discard things but to create a living space that fosters happiness and peace. She states, "The question of what you own is actually the question of how you want to live your life" (Kondo, 2014). Living with items and possessions soon reveals what we truly treasure.

Pope Francis has written,

"Christian spirituality proposes a growth marked by moderation and the capacity to be happy with little. It is a return to that simplicity which allows us to stop and appreciate the small things, to be grateful for the opportunities which life affords us, to be spiritually detached from what we possess, and not to succumb to sadness for what we lack." (Laudatio Si, 2015, #222).

Living Simply

Richard Foster (2005) offers practical themes for living more simply:

First, to buy only what is necessary and avoid luxury (Foster, p. 89-90, 2005). This goes against the flow of the next best thing. Rather, reflecting and pondering what is most critical and asking the question, "Do we really need things?" This is not being frugal but being mindful that our possessions possess us and that our decisions reflect who we are.

Second, to reject anything that produces addiction (Foster, p. 90, 2005). Smoking and Alcohol are easy to spot. But what about things we do day in and day out that provide entertainment? There is nothing intrinsically wrong with these things. But they may prevent us from living more fully in the present moment, in both the ups and the downs.

Third, develop a habit of giving things away (Foster, p. 90, 2005). This is so hard in a clutter-filled world. The need for more and more. This habit can help us to think, "What can I give away today?" Start with one thing each day. Can you do that? The hope is the realisation of not what I am lacking, but rather, how we can help another. As Jesus states: *"And if anyone wants to sue you and take your coat, give your cloak as well"* (Matthew 5:40). The realisation that other people are my brother or sister, not just biologically, but as a spiritual family that actively cares for the other.

Fourth, decrease reliance on credit and debt (Foster, p. 91, 2005). In Luke's Gospel, it was so hard for the rich man to let go of his riches (Chapter 18). Ultimate happiness is not found in the money in our bank accounts. Ultimate happiness allows us to appreciate what we already have. Our worry can decrease. We can stop trying to win a lottery, or desire to increase the price of our shares. Are we grateful for what we already have?

Fifth, reject materialism in advertising (Foster, p. 91, 2005). We need to be as cunning as wolves and as gentle as sheep (Matthew 10:16). Our TikTok or Facebook feed and TV Ads often create a façade of the perfect haircut or new iPhone. Materialism posits that goodness lies in our possessions. Our possessions can own us, so why don't we question what we see and appreciate what we already have?

Sixth, learn to enjoy simple pleasures (Foster, p. 90, 2005). There is joy in each and every moment. That joy can dazzle our senses. As we slowly eat a chocolate that sits on our tongue, do we appreciate the flavour? Do we rush? Slowing down allows us to enter more fully into the present moment, and we discover that this moment is unique. When we watch a small bird dance between trees in the morning air. This moment contains a deep joy that is infectious. As we close our eyes and breathe slowly, we speak God's name with each breath in and each breath out. The joy that we feel in each moment awakens us, so we can be aware that we are connected to something more.

Seventh, be intentional about clothing and fashion (Foster, p. 89, 2005). Do you shop at a big department store, prefer thrifting, or buy second-hand at a shop such as St Vincent de Paul or the Salvos? Second-hand clothing can make us appreciate something that someone else once loved. Thrifting supports recycling and can attune us to care for the earth. But not in excess, so we need to let go of some of our own clothes and give them away for others to love.

Eight, reduce waste and care for creation (Foster, p89-91, 2005). Recycling is not just about separating our waste into the correct bin. There are also recycling centres that specialise in electronic waste, soft plastics, paint, oils, glass, and so much more. Many organisations are seeking old books or old toys. Certainly, it takes a little effort to find them, but we can be part of the cycle that cares for creation with our hands and our feet simply by building our capacity to recycle.

Ninth, prioritise people over possessions (Foster, p. 89, 2005). We sometimes get caught up in our own thinking and our own need to do more and more and more. When we are on our deathbeds, it is not our possessions, which surround us, but the people we care about and who cared about us. There are people in our lives who will remember us from that time. How we care about them truly defines who we are. Our character and spirit grow when we face life's challenges together. We have a choice about whether to have gentle, loving, compassionate eyes, even though our ego sometimes wants to judge them. Quality time can be a doorway to bonding when we decide to step out of our own world and be present with the other.

Tenth, to seek God's Kingdom first (Foster, p. 91, 2005). The central point for the disciples and Jesus' followers of simplicity is to *"seek God's Kingdom and everything else will fall into a proper order"* (Matthew 6:33, NRSV). This can give us a vision that looks beyond our own small worldview and connects us with a hope that starts in our hearts and extends into the future. Every part is part of God's Kingdom. Like a thread in a tapestry or one piece of a puzzle, we can decide to do our part. This part does not belong to us. For this is part of God's life living in us.

Do we forget to live more fully present and aware of God's vision for us?

Often, moments in our lives can remind us of something more important happening beyond the endless cycle of our routines and patterns. The COVID lockdowns reminded us all to stop the relentless doing and step away from the constant cycle of making money and to climb the ladder of success. Some people chose not just to pause but to permanently leave their jobs. This marked the beginning of the great resignation. Employees who do not simply change jobs, but radically alter their lifestyles in the hope of achieving greater simplicity and meaning. We realized life isn't just about continuous work or our endless need for routine. In stopping, we uncovered something deeply significant, something spiritual. It is important to recognize that we do not always have to be busy or constantly productive. This is not the first time in human history that people have been enslaved by their work or oppressed by those in power who crushed the human spirit. We are reminded of the Jewish people's slavery in Egypt.

Exodus

In the Jewish tradition, there was an exodus some 3300 years ago where the Jewish people were freed from the slavery of constant work in Egypt.

It seems we may have forgotten this important story. After the Jewish people are freed from slavery, they soon receive God's law on Mount Sinai (Exodus 19-20, NRSV). The giving of God's law included a day of rest, the Sabbath, intended as a reminder to the Jews that they were freed from the slavery of relentless labour. Sadly, for many Christians today, it appears we've forgotten the value and significance of this day of rest.

Sabbath

The Orthodox Jewish people take the Sabbath very seriously. From sundown on Friday to sundown on Saturday, they pause completely, stopping all work. Orthodox Jews observe the 39 categories of prohibited activities detailed in the sacred book *"The Talmud"*, or *"Oral Torah"*. Orthodox Jewish people abstain from driving and refrain from using electronic devices such as phones. These 39 areas of activity are traditionally linked to the construction of their former sacred temple. Can we, too, learn something valuable from the Jewish people about regularly stopping each week?

Research supports the benefits of sabbath-keeping for mental and psychological health. A longitudinal study by Rae Jean Proeschold-Bell and colleagues found that increased frequency in Sabbath observance was associated with better mental health outcomes (2022). Similarly, research by Albert Cheng, Matthew Lee, and Rian Djata involving 1,300 teachers in Christian schools showed that Sabbath-keepers reported significantly lower levels of burnout, suggesting that Sabbath observance serves as a protective factor against professional exhaustion (2023).

Yet, didn't Jesus teach against the Sabbath? Arguing, *"The Sabbath was made for humankind, and not humankind for the Sabbath"* (Mark 2:27, NRSV)? Remember that the Sabbath was meant to liberate us from work and from slavery. Consider the context in which Jesus spoke in First Century Palestine. The Jewish people, especially the Pharisees, had become very rigid in their interpretation of the Sabbath and the Jewish laws. The spirit of the Sabbath, in that context and story, had been partially forgotten, as God intended it to be a day of liberation and mercy for people.

In Matthew's Gospel, we see Jesus heal a man with a withered hand on the Sabbath, in full view of the religious leaders, the Pharisees (12:9-13, NRSV). They were shocked, believing Jesus was breaking God's law. But Jesus was not focused merely on the letter of the law; He was concerned with the welfare of another. A higher principle was at play. The sacredness of human life and the call to restore someone to health. To liberate. To free one from the burden of suffering. Yet the religious leaders failed to see this deeper intent. Jesus' approach to the sabbath was radical at that time, but deeply rooted in compassion and mercy.

Jesus' keeping of the sabbath was not just about going to the synagogue (as it is for Christians today, going to church). Jesus would seek out places of rest. Jesus often would go into the wilderness to pray and seek solitude (Mark 1:35, NRSV). Jesus practised a spiritual discipline of withdrawing from the busyness of life (Luke 5:16, NRSV). Jesus would withdraw to escape the crowds (John 6:15, NRSV). In our own day, we need to travel into the desert and into the wilderness of our lives. Like Jesus, and get a taste of what stillness is really like. We should learn to make an active decision to down tools and enter the "in-between" time of the sabbath in our own lives. For instance, where we do not use our electronic devices. We can keep the sabbath for sharing and celebrating moments of quality family time together. We can have picnics on a rug, kick a ball in a park, and eat freshly made sandwiches. We should learn to set a specific day and time, commit to our new sabbath routine, and create the in-between time for stopping. As this is what Jesus modelled to us, not only to nurture a healthy spirituality but also a healthy life.

Margaret Diddams and her colleagues proposed a framework for Sabbath keeping (Diddams, Surdyk, Daniels, 2004). First, life segmentation, where individuals intentionally separate work from other aspects of life to create areas of respite. People need to set boundaries around work to avoid encroaching on personal and family time. Secondly, building meaning by incorporating positive, meaningful events and practices that renew and refresh us. Maybe church services may not always tick this box. Then we need to think creatively about how to bring God somehow into the practice of our lives. Finally, to integrate the sabbath, the sabbath is more deeply woven into different parts of our lives. We look forward to sabbath, but we also holistically build sabbath into moments when we need a spiritual awakening the most.

Journal

Spend 20 minutes journaling about the following.

Choose ONE of the following questions to journal about
1. *What does it mean to you to "leave the systems and pressures behind"? When have you experienced a moment of peace or connection in nature that awakened something spiritual in you?*

2. *What items would be in your metaphorical "backpack" for life's journey? Are they things that bring joy and purpose, or clutter and pressure?*

3. *Pope Francis spoke about the "capacity to be happy with little." What small things or simple pleasures in your life bring you joy or gratitude? How can you nurture those more intentionally?*

4. *In what ways do you currently observe rest or sabbath in your life? What practices could you introduce (or reintroduce) to set boundaries around busyness and reconnect with God and your loved ones in both everyday and each week?*

5. *Richard Foster invites us to "develop a habit of giving things away." What might you give away, a possession, a habit, or even your time, that could free you to live more simply?*

Journalling

Journalling

Journalling

Journalling

Prayer

Take a moment to pause.
 Close your eyes for two to three minutes.
 Become aware of your breathing.
 Breathe slowly.
 As you breathe in and as you breathe out.
 Afterwards, if it feels helpful, consider praying slowly this prayer in the days leading up to the next chapter.

Loving God,
in a world driven by noise, pressure, and endless doing, help us to pause, to walk the quieter path, and to rediscover the beauty of simplicity. Teach us to let go of what weighs us down, to cherish what truly matters, and to find joy in small moments of stillness and grace. May we seek Your Kingdom first, embrace moments of rest, and live lives that reflect Your joy, peace, generosity, and appreciation both for ourselves, our families, and the world around us.
Amen.

Pause

Pause for one day or one week before going to the next chapter.
    Allow the thoughts and ideas to sink in.
    Reflect.
    Ponder.
    Journal.
    Share with others.

Chapter Thirteen

Hope that brings a new beginning

Reflection – The puzzle pieces

"*Have you ever put a one-thousand-piece puzzle together? When we start, the box is filled with lots and lots of small pieces. Of different colours, sizes, and shapes.*

These pieces slowly get put together.
  It takes love to build a puzzle.
  It takes faith that they all fit together.
  It takes hope that one day the puzzle will be completed.

Maybe we can start by finding one corner of the picture.
   Maybe we can start by putting part of the puzzle together.

One day,
   as we sit at the table with the puzzle,
   when another person comes and sits down beside us,
   Maybe a family member,
   Maybe a friend,
   This can put a smile on our faces.
   The job of putting the puzzle together is made easier,
   When we work together.

Yet life is not always this simple.
   Sometimes we cannot fit the pieces together.
   Sometimes we lose pieces.
   Sometimes we hide pieces.
   Sometimes we avoid the ones that feel too painful to place.

And so the puzzle box gets pushed into the dark corner of our room,
   gathering dust, waiting for us to return.

But slowly, sometimes very slowly,
   We begin again.
   Piece by piece.
   Moment by moment.
   This takes commitment.
   This takes courage.

This takes the willingness to test, to try, and to trust which pieces truly belong.
  And over time, almost without noticing,
  a picture begins to appear.
  Beauty emerges where once there was only confusion.

Over time, we begin to see the beauty of the puzzle.
  The joy is not the end product.
  The joy is in the process of finding
  the pieces of the puzzle
  and how they fit together". (The author)

The puzzle is a symbol and metaphor for our own lives. We have deep questions that cross over the ordinary moments of our life. Questions that cannot be easily answered. Questions like *"why are we here? Is there an ultimate purpose and meaning to life? What happens when we die?"* Each of these questions is a puzzle. These puzzles are threaded through our lives. Christians believe that Jesus is the key part of the puzzle. Jesus is the cornerstone or the key through which reality makes sense.

But we may doubt?

Doubt can sometimes arise in our minds. After Jesus' resurrection, Thomas the Apostle doubted. He wanted proof of the resurrection. It may not be enough for someone to simply tell us, *"Have you heard? Some women from our group went early on Sunday morning, the eighth day of the week, carrying spices, expecting to find a body. But the Roman guards were gone, and the heavy stone had been rolled away. They entered the tomb only to find the cloth that had wrapped Jesus lying in a pile in the corner. As they left, they encountered two men dressed in white who said, 'Jesus has risen from the dead".* (Luke 24:1-7; Matthew 28:1-7; Mark 16:1-6; John 20:1-7, Paraphrased from NRSV)"

History Changes

Why is there a shift in human history following the events of the Resurrection? Shortly after, as the Acts of the Apostles describe in Acts Chapter 2, the story goes, the Holy Spirit was poured out at Pentecost, empowering the disciples to move beyond Jerusalem. But why did they need to go beyond Jerusalem? At the end of Mark's Gospel, Chapter 16, Jesus instructs his followers to *"Go out to all the world."* Some say that Thomas, the one who doubted the Resurrection, travelled all the way to India around 52AD (Medlycott, p. 6-10, 1905). Missionaries from Europe, arriving in India during the 12th, 13th, and 14th centuries, encountered an early Christian community claiming to have been founded by Saint Thomas the Apostle (Frykenberg, p. 111-113, 2008). But why would Thomas journey such a vast distance if he still doubted? Is this just a good story, or does it speak to something deeper, something transformative that changed even the most hesitant of hearts?

Martyrdom

Decades after the resurrection, the disciples Peter and Paul each made their way to Rome, where both met violent deaths. Early Christian tradition tells us that Peter was crucified upside down, and Paul was beheaded. If the resurrection were merely a fabricated story, why would these two men be willing to die for it? Around the same time, in approximately 64 AD, the Roman Emperor Nero outlawed Christianity throughout the Roman Empire. Being a Christian then carried a death sentence. Countless Christians were fed to lions or placed on poles as torch lamps in the

Colosseum as a public rejection of Christianity. This was a profound act of faith for the Christians, a testament to their unwavering belief in Jesus Christ. If the resurrection were false, why would so many continue to sacrifice their lives for it, not just in the decades following Jesus' death, but for centuries afterward? As the 2nd-century Christian writer Tertullian proclaimed, *"The blood of the martyrs is the seed of the Church"* (Tertullian, p. 171, 1958).

Not enough proof

Of course, this is still not enough evidence to definitively prove that Jesus rose from the dead. Sometimes, no matter how much evidence we uncover, we still don't have enough scientific or historical proof. With our modern, scientific mindset, these events simply don't make sense, and that's the point. It doesn't make sense. In ordinary life, when people die, they die. That is the natural order of things. Resurrection defies that order; it moves beyond what seems logical. But can we simply dismiss this as just a good story, or set it aside as something unimportant?

Not Optimism

The hope we seek is not the same as optimism. Optimism aims for specific outcomes and can often be measured; it is goal-oriented. But hope goes beyond any one person or personal achievement. Hope is a gift from God. As St. Paul writes, along with faith and love, hope is a virtue. Faith helps to activate the journey toward hope; it opens us up. Love allows hope to emerge; it motivates and connects us. And hope has the power to change reality. Yet, like children on Easter morning, we must go on an Easter egg hunt, a journey of discovery. The journey of faith is deeply personal, unique to each of our lives. Along the way, we may find suffering, doubt, and unexpected challenges. But the key is to step out into the deep, as Jesus says to the good thief, *"today you will be with me in paradise"* (Luke 23:43, NRSV), when Jesus calls us to go beyond what is logical or natural and to trust Him with our lives. Hope flourishes with both faith and love.

To believe in the resurrection, we must have a faith that lives in our own hearts. But the story does not begin with resurrection. Jesus' death preceded the resurrection. Jesus willingly handed himself over to die. This seems quite strange and raises questions in our hearts about why Jesus had to do that. We must look further back to see the pattern of why Jesus chose to die throughout his life. Throughout his ministry, Jesus actively chose to heal people who were sick both physically and spiritually. Jesus was known as a healer, not just simply because of what he knew or did not know, but because of the love that reigned in Jesus' heart. Jesus desired to care for those around him. He came to earth in order that we might know the love of God through our own lives. Today, during Advent, Christians are reminded to prepare and seek out Jesus not just in the past, but also in their own lives today. The Kingdom of God begins in the love that is in our hearts.

Personal Conversion

In Protestant and Pentecostal churches, personal conversion is considered a vital part of coming to faith in Jesus Christ. Each person is called to embark on a journey to discover, for themselves, a deeper truth, to have a personal encounter with the person of Jesus Christ. If Jesus Christ is truly alive today, some 2,000 years after the resurrection, does that not change everything? Does it not transform what is possible on life's journey?

In the Catholic Church, conversion is both personal and communal. The Catholic Church encourages conversion not only within the individual, but also in its mission (Catholic Church, #1428-1429, 1994). As the community lives out its call to bring the Good News of Jesus Christ to the world, it is hoped that it goes beyond itself and draws others in, including our family, our friends, and those on the outside. Conversion is deeply personal as each person can develop in their unique way. But conversion is also a lifelong and shared event. As we journey through life, we may discover a deeper understanding and experience of Jesus Christ and may continue to grow and change as Christians. This growth and these changes are made manifest in the community that we are a part of.

Breakthrough

The film Breakthrough (2019) tells the true story of 14-year-old John Smith in 2015, who fell through the ice of a frozen lake in Missouri and was trapped underwater for 15 minutes in the middle of winter. John was rescued and rushed to the hospital. While doctors fought to save him, his heart stopped for 45 minutes, and he was pronounced clinically dead. Left alone with her lifeless son, in tears, his mother Joyce offers a desperate prayer: *"Holy Spirit, if you are there, save my son."* She prays, prays, and prays. Miraculously, John's heart begins to beat again. Through Joyce's unfelt faith and the prayers of her friends and family, John's heart started to beat after 45 minutes without signs of life.

Can the power of faith in God bring people back to life?

Why does this not work with everyone?

We may not be able to answer these questions. Towards the end of the Breakthrough film (2019) John Smith is challenged by people who pose the question "Why me?" or *"Why was John Smith saved from dying?"* In an interview, John reflects that *"Yesterday is not ours to cover, but tomorrow is ours to win or lose"*. Hope is not something that can be achieved like optimism. Hope is a gift that moves beyond us.

Commitment

Soon after a baby is born in the Catholic and Orthodox churches, parents often baptize their children. The priest proclaims, *"I baptise you in the name of the Father, and of the Son, and of the Holy Spirit."* He then asks the parents and godparents, *"Do you promise to bring this child up in the faith?"* At such a young age, babies or children cannot declare their own faith. This requires a certain degree of reason and maturity. Parents, Godparents, and the wider Christian community are called to pass on the Christian tradition to these children. Like the disciples and saints who have gone before us, we learn about the Christian faith from them. We learn not by surface level information but by our lived experience of the Christian flame working in our own lives. But as the years go by, do these promises and faith commitments get left behind?

Do we leave our Christian faith at the altar, as life moves on to the next "better" thing? Like a gym membership, which seems important at first, but over time, we may lose that commitment to strengthen our faith. We can stop doing the spiritual "weights." But the spiritual life is so much more than a gym membership. This gym metaphor helps us to see where our priorities lie. Are we engaged in spiritual things? St Paul suggests that these spiritual things make sense only to those who are inspired by the Spirit (1 Corinthians 2:13-15), and that for those who are unspiritual, these things may seem foolish. Paul continues that we need to *"have the mind of Christ"* (1 Corinthians 2:13-15). That our actions, thoughts, and ideas are no longer our own. That we seek out a new perspective in life, which invokes God's Spirit to live through us. But for many Christians, unless it's Christmas or Easter, or when cultural expectations say otherwise, such as at weddings, we may not seek or desire to engage in spiritual things. Have we missed something here? In the first three centuries, in the early church, the spiritual life was centred around the home. Today, like a stale loaf of bread, we may lose the taste for being Christian.

Do we need something in our lives to wake us up to God's Spirit?

There are many examples of God's healing power throughout Church history. In 2010, the Catholic church officially recognised two medically unexplainable healings attributed to the intercession of Mary MacKillop (Mary MacKillop Canonisation and Recognised Healings Catholic News Service, 2010). The first involved a woman from the Central Coast in New South Wales who was diagnosed with terminal leukemia in the late 1960s. Her family and community prayed fervently for healing, and she made a complete recovery. The second occurred in the late 1990s, when a woman from Sydney suffering from terminal lung cancer also experienced healing after her community prayed through the intercession of Mary MacKillop. In the Catholic and Orthodox churches, it is believed that saints in Heaven can intercede and ask Jesus on behalf of those on Earth, even if they have died. However, such healings are not limited to the intercession of saints in Heaven. There are numerous examples of faith healings across all Christian traditions. The common thread in each case is faith in Jesus Christ. Pentecostal evangelist Smith Wigglesworth is said to have healed countless people through prayer alone, declaring, *"The power of God will take you through every storm and give you victory"* (Smith, 1997).

But in our own lives, should we depend solely on miracles or supernatural phenomena to sustain our faith? Or is there something even more powerful hidden within the ordinary moments that we often overlook? After Thomas witnessed the physical presence of the resurrected Jesus and touched the wounds in Jesus' side, in His body, where the Roman soldier had pierced Him. Jesus said, *"Have you believed because you have seen me? Blessed are those who have not seen and yet have come to believe"* (John 20:29, NRSV). The ordinary contains the greatest treasure where faith might be more fully realised. Rabbi Abraham Joshua Heschel once said, *"Our goal should be to live life in radical amazement. Get up in the morning and look at the world in a way that takes nothing for granted"* (Heschel, p. 11, 1976). Similarly, modern theologian Henri Nouwen wrote, *"The spiritual life does not remove us from the world but leads us deeper into it"* (Nouwen, p. 82, 1981). Our lives are more than they appear, because God is secretly woven into the fabric of each day.

Toward the end of both the Apostles' Creed and the Nicene Creed, we profess: *"We look for the resurrection of the dead."* This is not only about the resurrection of Jesus Christ but also about the transformation of our own lives. *"We look"* means you and me. Hope is not just hope. It is the hope that comes from Jesus Christ. What Jesus has done and continues to do in our lives today.

At the beginning of the Nicene Creed, Christians affirm belief in *"God, visible and invisible."* In this light, the invisible offers a profound opportunity to deepen our faith. When something seems absent, we are invited to become active instruments of God's grace. God can work through us if we are willing to let God in. With trust, even the most ordinary moment becomes a sacred space, open to God's transforming presence. This isn't about dramatic displays of divine power, but rather about the quiet, hidden ways God is present each day to each one of us. Every moment can become a profound encounter with the mystery of God. The ordinary lived experience of our lives is perhaps the greatest vehicle through which God's power is revealed, here and now. In the smallness. In the ordinary. In the parts people miss.

God waits at the door. In William Holman Hunt's painting *"The Light of the World,"* Jesus is depicted holding a lantern, representing the Light of the World (Hunt, 1853). He stands before a closed, overgrown door, symbolising the human heart. Notably, there is no handle on the outside; the handle is on the inside. It is from within our own lives that we must choose to open the door to God. As it says in Revelation 3:20: *"Behold, I stand at the door and knock. If anyone hears my voice and opens the door, I will come into him and eat with him, and he with me"* (NRSV). Are we willing to open the door? Do we recognize our need for God? In the darkness, sin, pain, challenge, hurt, brokenness, or illness that we may experience, God who offers us hope. In the end, the question remains: will we rekindle this Christian flame?

Journal

Spend 20 minutes journaling about the following.

Choose ONE of the following questions to journal about

1. What does the reflection on the puzzle pieces mean in your own life?

2. How does your faith in new life and hope help you face challenges and doubts in everyday life?

3. How is the heart and the faith which may live inside of it a doorway to seeking God? Give examples.

4. Where do you notice God quietly present in your ordinary, everyday moments?

5. What helps keep your sense of wonder and faith alive instead of letting it become routine?

6. How can hope help to transform your life?

Journalling

Journalling

Journalling

Journalling

Prayer

Take a moment to pause.
 Close your eyes for two to three minutes.
 Become aware of your breathing.
 Breathe slowly.
 As you breathe in and as you breathe out.
 Afterwards, if it feels helpful, consider praying slowly this prayer in the days leading up to the next chapter.

God of hope,
You are present not only in the miraculous but in the quiet rhythm of our days, in each breath, in each moment, in every unseen grace. Open our hearts to recognise your presence in the ordinary, that we may walk in wonder, listen in stillness, and live with the hope of the resurrection. Help us to trust, even when we do not see, and to believe, even when we do not fully understand. May your Spirit stir within us a deeper faith, a bolder love, and a renewed commitment to live as people of light, beyond our comfort, shaped not by fear or doubt, but by your unending grace. Amen.

Pause

Pause for one day or one week before going to the next chapter.

    Allow the thoughts and ideas to sink in.

    Reflect.

    Ponder.

    Journal.

    Share with others.

Chapter Fourteen

Conclusion

It has been many years since my dad asked my siblings and me to build a fire in our backyard. Now I am a dad, with children of my own. During winter, my wife often asks the kids to collect sticks and fallen branches from the park across the road. She'll say, "Should we go camping, even though it's freezing cold?" I usually say no. But maybe, just maybe, I'm missing something: the invitation to build the fire.

When we gather as a family around our little fire, something awakens in us, a spirit of warmth and connection in the darkness, as we roast marshmallows. Sometimes they burn. We have to be careful not to overcook them.

It's fascinating to watch the hot coals. When brought closer together, they burn more brightly. And it's the same with our Christian faith. We are called to come together. Jesus reminds us that where two or three are gathered in His name, He is present. We are invited to find those who resonate with our Christian spirit, not to stand passively on the sidelines, but to get our hands dirty, to pick up sticks, and stoke the Christian flame.

As Christians, we are called to go out into the world and spread the Good News. This mission begins in our homes, in the hidden dimensions of our daily lives. To live authentically means we cannot pretend to be Christians on Sunday and then forget the flame the rest of the time. Especially in the dark places of our lives. We are called to be the fire, awakening to God secretly woven into our lives.

We are like hot coals in the darkness, and we are called to seek out those still in the shadows. Not to wait for God to come to us. Not to wait for the poor to ask for help. But to be active in our faith like shepherds who search for the lost sheep (Matthew 18:12-14), like Jesus who goes to the woman at the well (John 4:4-42), to seek those on the margins. But paradoxically, this is not about adding more things, but doing the opposite. By moving from performance to presence, from status to service, from having more to having less. Tuning into the divine presence in our lives, we must learn to accompany others. To listen deeply. We must not impose our own agendas. It is not about taking centre stage, but about allowing God's gentle, relational, and humble way to have his way with us. By stepping back to simplify and subtract from our lives the things that distract us, we allow God's presence to come more fully into our own lives. We do not need to stand on street corners and forcefully demand that others follow. God's way is not our way. God's way is often hidden and unknown to others, but this is how the Christian flame begins.

God the Creator can work within us when we are willing to deeply listen to the voices in our lives and recognise God as both visible and invisible. In doing so, we allow God to shape more authentically who we are becoming.

It is not that we ignore the problems, hurts, and pains of life, but that we integrate them into the very fabric of the Christian flame. God chooses us and desires to embrace us completely, as His beloved children.

A final poem - Kindling the Christian Flame

"The winter night sky has come,
  Bringing the cold to our core,
  Problems of the past,
  Raising questions.
  Like water soaking our flames.
  The Christian light begins to dwindle.

  God calls out to us
  To rekindle the Christian flame
  Building a fire takes time.
  Gathering wood,
  Crunching paper,
  Making space.
  For something sacred to renew.

  Sometimes the Christian flame won't start.
  Sometimes it burns our hands.
  But with Spirit's wind,
  The fire finds a more proper form,
  And flickers into our lives.

  To rekindle the Christian Flame

It's for you to write the next chapter
of this book
in your own life.
To tend the Christian flame
into many shapes and forms.

In stillness, the flame begins again to light the night sky,
With courage,
With effort,
With awe.

When the hot coals are drawn together,
The fire grows stronger.

And when our own flame fades,
at the close of our days,
The Christian flame will burn on,
in hearts yet to be lit,
in lives yet to be warmed.

The Christian flame is not our flame.
It is God's flame.
A fire that never goes out". (The author)

Chapter Fifteen

Thank you

To the reader,

Thank you for journeying with me.

Your willingness to reflect, question, and open your heart is part of the same flame this book seeks to rekindle.

If this book has inspired you, I would be deeply grateful if you could take two minutes to share a short review online. Your words will help others discover their own spark and begin their journey to Rekindle the Christian Flame.

Click the link
https://www.andrewjohndumas.com/review

As You Go Out Into Your Life

May you continue to try new things,
   to listen deeply,
   and to inspire others to walk with you.
   May your presence bring light,
   and your actions reveal the love of God at work in the world.

One Final Prayer....

If it feels helpful, consider praying this final prayer slowly with me....

God, thank You for all that You have done
throughout our lives,
not only in the joyful moments,
but also in the difficult ones.
Teach us to seek You each day:
in our choices,
in our actions,
in our thoughts,
and in our feelings.

Inspire us to stop
and reflect.

Remind us to be
Your hands, Your feet, and Your heart
to all whom we meet. Amen.

Chapter Sixteen

Bibliography

Chapter 2

Anonymous. (2005). *The cloud of unknowing* (C. de Mello, Trans.). Image Books. (Original work published ca. 14th century)

Bonhoeffer, D. (1997). *Letters and Papers from Prison* (J. de Gruchy, Ed.; R. H. Fuller & F. Clark, Trans.). Touchstone. (Original work published 1951)

Frankl, V. E. (2006). *Man's search for meaning* (I. Lasch, Trans.). Beacon Press. (Original work published 1946.

Luther, M. (2005). *The bondage of the will* (J. I. Packer & O. R. Johnston, Trans.). Revell. (Original work published 1525)

Rohr, R., Finley, J., & Bourgeault, C. (2010). *Following the mystics through the narrow gate: Seeing God in all things* [Audio course]. Center for Action and Contemplation.

Wiesel, E. (2006). *Night* (M. Wiesel, Trans.). Hill and Wang. (Original work published 1956)

Chapter 3

Chapman, B., Hickner, S., & Wells, S. (Directors). (1998). *The prince of Egypt* [Film]. DreamWorks Animation.

Lewis, C. S. (1960). *The four loves*. London, England: Geoffrey Bles.

Rohr, R., Finley, J., & Bourgeault, C. (2010). *Following the mystics through the narrow gate: Seeing God in all things* [Audio course]. Center for Action and Contemplation.

Chapter 4

Benedict XVI. (2005, August 18). *Address to the volunteers at World Youth Day*. Cologne, Germany. Libreria Editrice Vaticana. https://www.vatican.va/content/benedict-xvi/en/speeches/2005/august/documents/hf_ben-xvi_spe_20050818_wyd-volunteers.html

Cassavetes, N. (Director). (2004). *The Notebook* [Film]. New Line Cinema.

Einstein, A. (1941). *Science, philosophy and religion: A symposium*. New York, NY: Conference on Science, Philosophy and Religion in Their Relation to the Democratic Way of Life, Inc.

Peck, M. S. (1990). *The road less travelled: A new psychology of love, traditional values and spiritual growth*. Arrow Books. (Original work published 1978)

McNamara, S. (Director). (2011). *Soul surfer* [Film]. TriStar Pictures.

Rohr, R. (2003). *Everything belongs: The gift of contemplative prayer*. New York, NY: Crossroad Publishing.

Rohr, R. (2005). *Adam's return: The five promises of male initiation*. Crossroad Publishing.

Rohr, R., Finley, J., & Bourgeault, C. (2010). *Following the mystics through the narrow gate: Seeing God in all things* [Audio course]. Center for Action and Contemplation..

Chapter 5

Brueggemann, W. (1978). *The Prophetic Imagination*. Fortress Press.

Hederman, M. P. (2008). *The opal and the pearl: The renewed life of Vatican II*. Columba Press.

Joffé, R. (Director). (1986). *The mission* [Film]. Warner Bros.

Muccino, G. (Director). (2006). *The pursuit of happyness* [Film]. Columbia Pictures.

Payne, A., Coen, J., Coen, E., Cuaron, A., Park, C. W., Tykwer, T., ... & Téchiné, A. (Directors). (2006). *Paris, je t'aime* [Film]. Victoires International, La Fabrique de Films.

Peck, M. S. (1990). *The road less travelled: A new psychology of love, traditional values and spiritual growth*. Arrow Books. (Original work published 1978).

Chapter 6

60 Minutes Australia. (2011, October 23). *Emmanuel Kelly: Born to perform* [Video]. YouTube. https://www.youtube.com/watch?v=CxP0xb7Odj8

Benedict XVI. (2005, August 21). *Homily at the conclusion of World Youth Day*, Cologne, Germany. Libreria Editrice Vaticana. https://www.vatican.va

Brown, B. (2012). *Daring greatly: How the courage to be vulnerable transforms the way we live, love, parent, and lead*. Gotham Books.

Ellsberg, R. (1992). *Dorothy Day: A biography*. HarperOne.

Hollis, J. (2003). *Finding meaning in the second half of life: How to finally, really grow up*. Gotham Books.

Jackson, M. (Director). (1999). *Tuesdays with Morrie* [TV movie]. Harpo Films; Carlton America; American Broadcasting Company.

Palmer, P. J. (2000). *Let your life speak: Listening for the voice of vocation*. Jossey-Bass.

Perel, E. (2006). *Mating in captivity: Unlocking erotic intelligence*. Harper.

Rogers, C. R. (1961). *On becoming a person: A therapist's view of psychotherapy*. Houghton Mifflin.

Vatican News. (2025). *St. Gianna Beretta Molla: Patron saint of mothers, physicians, and unborn children*. Retrieved April 13, 2025, from https://www.vaticannews.va/en/saints/04/28/st--gianna-beretta-molla--wife--mother--doctor.html

Chapter 7

Al-Ghazali. (1993). *The revival of religious learnings* (Ihya' 'Ulum al-Din) (Fazl-ul-Karim, Trans.; Vol. 1). Darul-Ishaat. (Original work published ca. 1100)

Anselm of Canterbury. (n.d.). *Stanford Encyclopedia of Philosophy*. Retrieved from https://plato.stanford.edu/entries/anselm/

Catherine of Siena. (1980). *The dialogue* (S. Noffke, Trans.). Paulist Press. (Original work published 1378)

D'Arcy, P. (1996). *Gift of the red bird: The story of a divine encounter*. Crossroad.

Doss, D., & Drummond, B. (2005). *The unlikeliest hero: The story of Desmond T. Doss, conscientious objector who won his nation's highest military honour*. Pacific Press Publishing Association.

European Space Agency. (n.d.). *The dark Universe*. Retrieved from https://www.esa.int/Science_Exploration/Space_Science/Euclid/The_dark_Universe :contentReference{index=10}

Frankl, V. E. (2006). *Man's search for meaning* (I. Lasch, Trans.). Beacon Press. (Original work published 1946)

Gibson, M. (Director). (2016). *Hacksaw Ridge* [Film]. Summit Entertainment.

John of the Cross. (1959). *Dark night of the soul* (E. A. Peers, Trans.; 3rd rev. ed.). Image Books/Doubleday. (Original work published ca. 1578)

Jung, C. G. (1979). *Aion: Researches into the phenomenology of the self* (R. F. C. Hull, Trans.). Princeton University Press. (Original work published 1951)

Kerr, A. (2009). *Catherine of Siena: Spiritual development in her life and teaching*. Paulist Press.

Prodigal Catholic. (2019, May 31). *Summary of The Dark Night of the Soul by St. John of the Cross*.

Ward, V. (Director). (1998). *What dreams may come* [Film]. PolyGram Filmed Entertainment; Universal Pictures.

Chapter 8

Dawkins, R. (1995). *River out of Eden: A Darwinian view of life*. Basic Books.

Frankl, V. E. (2006). *Man's search for meaning* (I. Lasch, Trans.). Beacon Press. (Original work published 1946)

King, M. L., Jr. (1963). *Strength to love*. Harper & Row.

Wiesel, E. (2006). *Night* (M. Wiesel, Trans.). Hill and Wang. (Original work published 1956)

Chapter 9

Adamson, A., & Jenson, V. (Directors). (2001). *Shrek* [Film]. DreamWorks Pictures.

Augustine. (1961). *Confessions* (R. S. Pine-Coffin, Trans.). Penguin Books. (Original work published ca. 397-400 CE)

Augustine. (1887). *Sermon 72: On prayer and fasting* (De oratione et jejunio). In P. Schaff (Ed.), A select library of the Nicene and Post-Nicene Fathers of the Christian Church, First Series (Vol. 6, pp. 345–346). Christian Literature Publishing Co. (Original work published ca. 4th–5th century)

Chbosky, S. (Director). (2012). *The perks of being a wallflower* [Film]. Summit Entertainment.

Habig, M. A. (Ed.). (1973). *St. Francis of Assisi: Writings and early biographies*. English omnibus of sources (rev. ed.). Franciscan Herald Press.

Van Sant, G. (Director). (1997). *Good Will Hunting* [Film]. Miramax Films.

Chapter 10

Hazeldine, S. (2017). *The shack* [Film]. Summit Entertainment.

Jenkins, D. (2017–present). *The chosen* [TV series]. Angel Studios.

Kraybill, D. B., Nolt, S. M., & Weaver-Zercher, D. L. (2007). *Amish grace: How forgiveness transcended tragedy*. San Francisco, CA: Jossey-Bass.

Origen. (1966). *On first principles* (G. W. Butterworth, Trans.). Harper & Row. (Original work published ca. 220 CE)

Phan Thi, K. P. (2017). *Fire Road: The Napalm Girl's Journey through the Horrors of War to Faith, Forgiveness, and Peace*. Tyndale House Publishers.

Sidwell, V. (2007, October 14). *In The Abbey* (Documentary series). ABC TV. Australia.

Chapter 11

Augustine. (n.d.). Sermon 299D. In J. E. Rotelle (Ed.), *The works of Saint Augustine: A translation for the 21st century* (Vol. III/8, Sermons). New City Press.

Bouchareb, R. (Producer), & Troch, P. (Director). (1999). *Molokai: The story of Father Damien* [Film]. Kinepolis Film Distribution.

Hallie, P. (1979). *Lest innocent blood be shed: The story of the village of Le Chambon and how goodness happened there*. Harper & Row.

Hancock, J. L. (2009). *The blind side* [Film]. Warner Bros. Pictures.

Leder, M. (Director). (2000). *Pay it forward* [Film]. Warner Bros.

Long, V. (2021, June 30). *Bishop Vincent: 'My hope for the Plenary Council'*. Catholic Outlook. https://catholicoutlook.org/bishop-vincent-my-hope-for-the-plenary-council/

Chapter 12

Cheng, A., Lee, M. H., & Djita, R. (2023). *A cross-sectional analysis of the relationship between Sabbath practices and US, Canadian, Indonesian, and Paraguayan teachers' burnout*. Journal of Religion and Health, 62(2), 1090–1113. https://doi.org/10.1007/s10943-022-01647-w

Diddams, M., Surdyk, L. K., & Daniels, D. (2004). *Rediscovering models of Sabbath keeping: Implications for psychological well-being*. Journal of Psychology and Theology, 32(1), 3–11.

Estevez, E. (Director). (2010). *The way* [Film]. Elixir Films; Filmax; Icon Entertainment International.

Foster, R. J. (2005). *Celebration of discipline: The path to spiritual growth* (25th anniversary ed.). HarperSanFrancisco. (Original work published 1978)

Kondo, M. (2014). *The life-changing magic of tidying up: The Japanese art of decluttering and organizing* (C. Hirano, Trans.). Ten Speed Press.

Kondo, M. (Host). (2019). *Tidying up with Marie Kondo* [TV series]. Netflix.

Pope Francis. (2015). *Encyclical Letter Laudato Si' of the Holy Father Francis on care for our common home*. Accessed on June 1 2025 from https://www.vatican.va/content/francesco/en/encyclicals/documents/papa-francesco_20150524_enciclica-laudato-si.html

Proeschold-Bell, R. J., Stringfield, B., Yao, J., Choi, J., Eagle, D., Hybels, C. F., Parnell, H., Keefe, K., & Shilling, S. (2022). *Changes in Sabbath-keeping and mental health over time: Evaluation findings from the Sabbath Living Study*. Journal of Psychology and Theology, 50(2), 123–138. https://doi.org/10.1177/00916471211046227

Chapter 13

Catholic Church. (1994). *Catechism of the Catholic Church* (2nd ed.). Vatican City: Libreria Editrice Vaticana

Frykenberg, R. E. (2008). *Christianity in India: From beginnings to the present*. Oxford University Press.

Heschel, A. J. (1976). *God in Search of Man: A Philosophy of Judaism*. Farrar, Straus and Giroux.

Hunt, W. H. (1853). *The Light of the World* [Painting]. Keble College, Oxford, England.

Mary MacKillop Canonisation and Recognised Healings Catholic News Service. (2010, October 17). *Pope canonizes Australia's first saint, Mary MacKillop*. Retrieved from https://www.catholicnews.com

Medlycott, A. E. (1905). *India and the Apostle Thomas: An inquiry, with a critical analysis of the Acts Thomas*. David Nutt.

Nouwen, H. J. M. (1981). *Making All Things New: An Invitation to the Spiritual Life*. Harper & Row.

Smith Wigglesworth Polhill, J. B. (1997). *The centennial history of Pentecostalism*. Baker Books.

Tertullian. (197 A.D./1958). *Apologeticus* (T. R. Glover, Trans.). In T. R. Glover & G. H. Whitaker (Eds.), Tertullian: Apology. De Spectaculis (pp. 1–135). Harvard University Press. (Original work published ca. 197 A.D.)

www.ingramcontent.com/pod-product-compliance
Lightning Source LLC
Chambersburg PA
CBHW020108240426
43661CB00002B/80